EMBRACED
BY MERCY

God's Ultimate Gift

Jim McManus C.Ss.R.

Published by **Redemptorist Publications**
Alphonsus House, Chawton, Hampshire, GU34 3HQ, UK
Tel. +44 (0)1420 88222, Fax. +44 (0)1420 88805
Email rp@rpbooks.co.uk, www.rpbooks.co.uk

A registered charity limited by guarantee
Registered in England 3261721

Copyright © Redemptorist Publications 2015
First published November 2015

Edited by Sr Thérèse Garman
Designed by Christine Reissland

ISBN 978-0-85231-447-0

A CIP catalogue record for this book is available from the British Library.

The publisher gratefully acknowledges permission to use the following copyright material:

Excerpts from the English translation and chants of *The Roman Missal*.

© 2010, International Commission on English in the Liturgy Corporation. All rights reserved.

Excerpts from *The Jerusalem Bible*, copyright © 1966 by Darton, Longman & Todd, Ltd and Doubleday, a division of Random House, Inc. Reprinted by permission.

New Jerusalem Bible, copyright © 1994 by Darton, Longman & Todd Ltd.

Excerpts from the New Revised Standard Version of the Bible: Anglicised Edition, © 1989. 1995, Division of Christian Education of the National Council of the Churches of Christ in the United States of America. Used by permission. All rights reserved.

Excerpts from Vatican Council II: The Basic Sixteen Documents (Northport, NY: Costello, 1966) by Reverend Austin Flannery OP.

Psalms from the Grail Psalter reprinted by permission of HarperCollins Publishers Ltd © 1963.

Front cover: "Le Fils Prodigue" by Arcabas, used with permission.

Printed by Bishops Printers Limited, Portsmouth PO6 1TR

Dedication

As I wrote this book on God's great mercy I was thanking the Lord for my five nieces Emer, Jacinta, Sharon, Sinead and Edel, and for my fifteen nephews Gerard, Patrick, Peter, Michael, Patrick, Sean, Brian, Crosby, Thomas, Seamus, Ronan, Fergal, James, Barry and Myles. I dedicate this book in gratitude to them for their love, friendship and generosity to me over the years.

— Contents —

— Introduction —

A new language

Pope Francis, in promulgating the Jubilee Year of Mercy, said, "It is absolutely essential for the Church and for the credibility of her message that she herself live and testify to mercy. Her language and her gestures must transmit mercy, so as to touch the hearts of all people and inspire them once more to find the road that leads to the Father."[1] He is calling on the Church to use the language of mercy which alone can communicate the joy of the Gospel in new ways to the people of our time. When people encounter the Church they should encounter the mercy of God. As Pope Francis says:

> Wherever the Church is present, the mercy of the Father must be evident. In our parishes, communities, associations and movements, in a word wherever there are Christians, everyone should find the oasis of mercy.[2]

St John XXIII, in his opening speech to the Second Vatican Council in 1962, stated very clearly that what the people of God, the Church, most needed in the 1960s was "a new enthusiasm, a new joy and serenity of mind in the unreserved acceptance of the entire Christian faith". This new enthusiasm and joy were needed to defend against what St John XXIII called the "prophets of gloom, who are always forecasting disaster, as though the end of the world were at hand".[3] There have been "prophets of doom" in every age of the Church and, even though St John XXIII acknowledged that they "were burning with zeal" for the Church, their message was one of discouragement, the very opposite of the message which should go out to the whole

---

1   Pope Francis, Misericordiae Vultus: *Bull of Indiction of the Extraordinary Jubilee Year of Mercy*, 12
2   *Ibid*
3   St John XXIII, Opening Speech to the Second Vatican Council, 15

world from the Council, namely, one of hope. As the Council would teach, "One is right in thinking that the future of humanity rests with people who are capable of providing the generations to come with reasons for living and reasons for hoping."[4]

St John XXIII knew that the Council would review the whole of Christian tradition and from the richness of the Church's doctrine would give the message of hope, the Gospel of hope, to the modern world. To facilitate a wide ranging exploration, he made a very important distinction when he reminded the bishops that:

> The deposit of faith, or truths which are contained in our time-honoured teaching, is one thing; the manner in which these truths are set forth (with their meaning preserved intact) is something else.[5]

The Church is not tied to ancient formulas or any particular philosophical approach when explaining the doctrines of our faith. The Church should always speak to the faithful in a language that even the least educated can easily understand. St John XXIII, himself a very brilliant man, was the son of a small farmer in Lombardy, Italy, the fourth of fourteen children. He never forgot how to speak to the farming men and women of the countryside who never had the opportunity of a university education.

The medicine of mercy

As Pope, he wanted the Church to communicate the Gospel of Christ with clarity of thought and simplicity of language. Most of all, he wanted the Church to bring to people a real experience of God's mercy. He outlined the new approach that he wished the Council to take with these words:

> The Church has always opposed errors, and often condemned them with the utmost severity. Today, however,

---

4   Constitution on the Church in the Modern World, 31
5   Opening Speech, 15

Christ's Bride prefers the medicine of mercy to the arm of severity. She believes that present needs are best served by explaining more fully the purport of her doctrines, rather than by publishing condemnations.[6]

Those two short statements about "the medicine of mercy" and expressing old truths in new ways have reverberated throughout the Church during the past fifty years. Today Pope Francis has made "the medicine of mercy" the major theme of his pontificate.

Successive popes took up the theme of a new language. Blessed Paul VI, who succeeded St John XXIII, wrote in his first encyclical that the Church in her dialogue "does not hold fast to forms of expression which have lost their meaning and can no longer stir people's minds".[7] He recognised that theological explanations of Gospel truths which were full of meaning for one generation may have little meaning for a new generation, not because the truth has lost its meaning, but because the language in which the truth is expounded "no longer stirs minds". Benedict XVI was very alert to this phenomenon of how language that was once helpful can lose its power to communicate. Speaking about the truth of the Second Coming of Christ he pointed out:

> The Gospel has been presented in formulas that, while true, are nevertheless at the same time outmoded. They no longer speak to our living situation and are no longer comprehensible to us.[8]

And Pope Francis wrote:

> There are times when the faithful, in listening to completely orthodox language, take away something alien to the authentic Gospel of Jesus Christ, because that language is alien to their own way of speaking to and understanding one another.[9]

---

6   *Ibid* 16
7   Blessed Paul VI, *Ecclesiam Suam*, 1964, para 85
8   Benedict XVI, *Of the World*, Catholic Truth Society, 2010, p. 63
9   Pope Francis, *The Joy of the Gospel*, 46

Our great challenge today is to speak the truths which the Church teaches us, in a language that we ourselves, and those to whom we are speaking, can understand. Pope Francis helps us with this because he has a very clear vision of what the Church needs in our time. He writes:

> I see clearly that the thing the Church needs most today is the ability to heal wounds and to warm the hearts of the faithful; it needs nearness, proximity. I see the Church as a field hospital after battle. It is useless to ask a seriously injured person if he has high cholesterol and about the level of his blood sugar! You have to heal his wounds. Then we can talk about everything else.[10]

He is taking his cue from St John XXIII. He is speaking a language, both in his homilies and in his writings, that every person can easily understand. He sees the Church as a "field hospital" where the Church ministers the "medicine of mercy" for the healing of her wounded children, our wounded society and indeed our wounded world.

Francis, from his very first day as Pope, has been proclaiming God's mercy and calling the whole Church back to the awareness that God is "the Father of mercies and the God of all consolation" (2 Corinthians 1:2). God, he keeps reminding us, never tires of forgiving us: we tire of asking for forgiveness. He now invites the whole Church to celebrate an Extraordinary Jubilee Year of Mercy. This will be a grace for the whole Church and indeed for the whole world. In the opening words of his Bull of Indiction proclaiming the Jubilee he writes:

> Jesus Christ is the face of the Father's mercy. These words might well sum up the mystery of the Christian faith. Mercy has become living and visible in Jesus of Nazareth, reaching its culmination in him. The Father,

---

10 Pope Francis, Interview in *America* Magazine, 30 September 2013

"rich in mercy" (Ephesians 2:4), after having revealed his name to Moses as "a God merciful and gracious, slow to anger, and abounding in steadfast love and faithfulness" (Exodus 34:6), has never ceased to show, in various ways throughout history, his divine nature.[11]

Pope Francis has the profound, indeed prophetic, awareness that we are living in a special time of God's mercy and he sees that his specific mission is to awaken in the whole Church, and indeed the whole world, this awareness: Jesus Christ is the face of the Father's mercy. Our world needs to hear this truth, but also our Church needs to renew her faith in this truth, because our awareness of the mercy of God can grow dim. At times we have been tempted to place law before mercy and justice before love, forgetting the great Gospel truth that God's justice is his mercy and God's law is the law of love. Pope Francis outlines his hopes for this Jubilee of Mercy in the second paragraph of his proclamation:

> We need constantly to contemplate the mystery of mercy. It is a wellspring of joy, serenity, and peace. Our salvation depends on it. Mercy: the word reveals the very mystery of the Most Holy Trinity. Mercy: the ultimate and supreme act by which God comes to meet us. Mercy: the fundamental law that dwells in the heart of every person who looks sincerely into the eyes of his brothers and sisters on the path of life. Mercy: the bridge that connects God and man, opening our hearts to the hope of being loved forever despite our sinfulness.[12]

We must take very seriously Pope Francis' appeal to the Church to begin a deeper reflection on the mercy of God and to live God's mercy in all our relationships. The title I have chosen for this short book is *Embraced by Mercy: God's Ultimate Gift*. Since, in the words of Pope Francis, "Jesus Christ is the face of the Father's mercy",

---

11 Pope Francis, Misercordiae Vultus: Bull of Indiction of the Extraordinary Jubilee Year of Mercy, 1
12 *Ibid* 2

to be embraced by mercy means to be embraced by Jesus Christ. It is in Christ's embrace of mercy and love that each of us finds our salvation. My hope is that this little book will help you to experience in new ways this wonderful grace of God's mercy in your own life and see this mercy touch and renew the lives of all your loved ones.

In the first chapter we will reflect on St Bernard's great insight, and one frequently quoted by Pope Francis: the mercy of God is my merit. This will give us the opportunity to become more aware of the many subtle ways in which we can misunderstand God's mercy and deprive ourselves of inner peace.

In the second chapter we will look at how Jesus teaches us to understand God's mercy in his great stories that we call his parables. You may have often heard the saying that "a picture is worth a thousand words". The parables of Jesus on the mercy of God the Father are worth more than a thousand books.

In the third chapter we will look in some depth at how St Paul who called himself the greatest of all sinners received the mercy and forgiveness of God.

In the fourth chapter we will begin applying the good news of the mercy of God to ourselves. Jesus tells us, "Blessed are the merciful for they shall have mercy shown them" (Matthew 5:8). He also gives us this commandment, "Be merciful as your heavenly Father is merciful" (Luke 6:36).

In the fifth, sixth and seventh chapters we will reflect on the powerful means that Jesus has given to us so that we can be as merciful as our heavenly Father. He has given us his sacraments in which we meet him personally every time we approach the throne of mercy in the sacrament of confession, each time we come to the altar of the Lord to celebrate and participate in the Holy Mass and, when we are sick, each time we open our hearts to receive the holy anointing in the sacrament of the sick.

In the final chapter we will turn our attention to Our Lady whom the Church calls the Mother of Mercy and whom we honour as our Mother of Perpetual Succour.

At the end of each chapter, I will invite you to enter into the quietness of your own heart and be still with the God of mercy who makes his home in you. This will be a moment for interiorising the main message of each chapter. It will help you to get the message from your head into your heart.

I am most grateful to the staff and editors at Redemptorist Publications for publishing this book.

Jim McManus C.Ss.R.

— Chapter One —

The mercy of God is my merit

The first time I read the words of the great St Bernard, "the mercy of God is my merit", it dawned on me that here we have the answer to the problem so many of us have in really accepting that God loves us and that we are "precious in God's sight" (Isaiah 43:4). In our own experience we are conscious of the struggle we have between good and evil, between loving and rejecting, and that includes loving ourselves and rejecting ourselves. Deep down we are conscious that we are sinners, that we are selfish despite all our efforts to be generous and loving. And, somehow, the awareness of how we fall short can blind us to the many ways in which we rise above ourselves and give ourselves generously to others. Then, instead of thanking God for the many ways in which "the Spirit comes to help us in our weakness" (Romans 8:26) we secretly condemn ourselves and even reject ourselves. We begin to turn the "good news" that we are "sinners whom God loves" into the reason why we have to reject ourselves because we are sinners. Instead of rejoicing in God's great mercy, we allow negativity about ourselves to enter our souls and we begin to lose the joy of the Gospel. In the very first line of his famous *Exhortation on The Joy of the Gospel*, Pope Francis reminds us that,

> The joy of the Gospel fills the hearts and lives of all who encounter Jesus. Those who accept his offer of salvation are set free from sin, sorrow, inner emptiness and loneliness. With Christ joy is constantly renewed.[1]

---

1   Pope Francis, *The Joy of the Gospel*, 1

The encounter with Jesus is an encounter with mercy because, as Pope Francis says, "Jesus Christ is the face of the Father's mercy".[2]

Joy is constantly renewed as we accept and welcome the mercy of God into our hearts and we share that mercy with others.

St Paul had to remind the Ephesians that they cannot save themselves:

> God loved us with so much love that he was generous with his mercy: when we were dead through our sins, he brought us to life with Christ - it is through grace that you have been saved, through faith; not by anything of your own, but by a gift from God; not by anything that you have done, so that nobody can claim the credit. We are God's work of art, created in Christ Jesus to live the good life as from the beginning he had meant us to live it (Ephesians 2:4-6, 8-10).

Our most subtle sin is, I often think, "claiming the credit" for the good that we do and failing to acknowledge that, "It is God, for his own loving purpose, who puts both the will and the action into you" (Philippians 2:13). If we forget this great truth of our salvation we will end up finding fault with the people who don't do the same good works that we do, criticising others for the lives they are living and ignoring the clear warning of Jesus, "cut off from me you can do nothing" (John 15:5).

We cannot take the credit for the good works we do, because without the grace of God we would not be able to do them. The Blessed Virgin Mary teaches us how to acknowledge God's working in our lives: "My soul proclaims the greatness of the Lord and my spirit exults in God my saviour...For the Almighty has done great things for me, Holy is his name" (Luke 1:49). God does great things in all our lives. We are not being humble if we refuse to acknowledge God's grace. But attributing to ourselves the credit for the good works that God in his mercy enables us to do is surely the real sin of pride.

---

2   Pope Francis, Bull of Indiction of the Jubilee Year of Mercy, 1

Love is unmerited

The sin of pride robs us of the experience of receiving love as freely given, totally unmerited. We cannot earn love. Nor can we persuade anyone to love us. Pride seeks to instil in us the false sense that we must deserve the love of others before we can receive it. Then, when we receive the love, we can lay claim to it on the mistaken grounds that we deserve it. This sneaking need in us to feel that we have merited the love in some way becomes the great enemy of love because it undermines the wonder of the free gift that is being offered to us. This false understanding of meriting love undermines any real intimacy with God. Deep down in our hearts we know that we cannot merit the love of God. Sin then begins to whisper in our inner ear that because we are sinners, incapable of meriting love, God could never love us. And, since we cannot merit God's love we can never be close to God and we can never really be precious in his sight. This false reasoning can be summed up in this way: love has to be merited; the sinner can never merit God's love, therefore the sinner can never be loved by God. St Bernard responds to this false thinking with these powerful words,

> For my part, what I lack of myself I confidently take to myself from the compassionate heart of the Lord which flows with mercy and which is provided with outlets through which mercy flows... The mercy of the Lord is, then, my merit. I am never bereft of merit as long as he is not bereft of mercy. For if the mercies of the Lord are many, then many are my merits. But what if I am aware of my many sins? Then where sin increased, grace abounded all the more. And if the steadfast love of the Lord is from everlasting to everlasting, then I will sing of the steadfast love of the Lord for ever. And what of my own righteousness? "Lord, I shall be mindful only of your righteousness. For your righteousness is also mine since you have been made my righteous by God".[3]

---

3   Office of Readings, Wednesday, Week 3

We have infinite merit because the mercy of God is our merit. That means God loves us infinitely, not because we are holy but because he wants to share his own holiness with us. St Paul expressed all this in a nutshell when he wrote to Titus:

> When the kindness and love of God our saviour for mankind were revealed, it was not because he was concerned with any righteous action we might have done ourselves; it was for no reason except his own compassion that he saved us, by means of the cleansing water of rebirth and by renewing us with the Holy Spirit which he has so generously poured over us through Jesus Christ our saviour. He did this so that we should be justified by his grace, to become heirs looking forward to inheriting eternal life. This is doctrine that you can rely on (Titus 3:4-8).

We cannot redeem ourselves. Redemption is the gift of Christ. It is the manifestation of the unconditional love of God our Father who is, in the words of St Paul, "a gentle Father and the God of all consolation" (2 Corinthians 1: 3). God our Father knows that we are sinners. It is as sinners that we are loved by God. As St Paul says, "What proves that God loves us is that Christ died for us while we were still sinners" (Romans 5:8). God meets us in our sinful state and in his great mercy he reconciles us with himself. Through his mercy we are, as Jesus says, "born again through water and the Spirit" (John 3:5). We have to allow this truth to sink into the core of our being: God loves me, not because I am holy but because he wants to share his love and holiness with me. We can never deserve to be loved in that way. When we open our heart gratefully to receive the free gift of God's infinite love our hearts become new, our whole being is renewed. That is God's great promise to his people:

> I shall pour clean water over you and you will be cleansed;
> I shall cleanse you of all your defilement and all your idols.
> I shall give you a new heart, and put a new spirit in you;

I shall remove the heart of stone from your bodies and give you a heart of flesh instead. I shall put my spirit in you, and make you keep my laws and sincerely respect my observances. You will live in the land which I gave your ancestors. You shall be my people and I shall be your God (Ezekiel 36:25-29).

It is all God's gift

From the very depths of our being, as the cleansing and purifying mercy of God washes over us, we have to give thanks. God's love purifies us from all our sins and makes us holy in God's sight. Now we gratefully accept ourselves and in the words of the psalm we can say to God,

It was you who created my inmost self,
and put me together in my mother's womb;
for all these mysteries I thank you;
for the wonder of myself, for the wonder of all your works
(Psalm 139:13-14).

God teaches us individually to thank him for "the wonder of myself". In doing so we are thanking him for the wonder of his creation and of our redemption. We can surely say with St Bernard: "Thank you; your mercy is my merit." Now I no longer hold on to the guilt of sins that the Lord has forgiven. And I no longer feel the need to condemn myself because I am a sinner. When Pope Francis was asked in an interview, "who is Pope Francis?" he said, "I am a sinner whom the Lord regards". All our great saints were deeply aware that they were sinners, but this consciousness of sinfulness didn't depress them or make them reject themselves. Rather, it filled them with joy because every day their trust was not in their own good works but in Jesus Christ who had come to save them from their sins. They could praise God "for the wonder of themselves" because they believed with St Bernard that the mercy of God was their merit.

Living by the life-giving word of God

Jesus says to us that we live "on every word that comes from the mouth of God" (Matthew 4:4). Consider the liberating power of this word that God speaks to us poor sinners through the prophet Isaiah:

> Come now, let us talk this over,
>   says the Lord.
> Though your sins are like scarlet,
>   they shall be as white as snow;
> though they are red as crimson,
>   they shall be like wool (Isaiah 1:18).

This transformation of our sins into holiness when we "talk over our life" with God, reveals to us who our God truly is. As the psalm says, "The Lord is compassion and love, slow to anger and rich in mercy" (Psalm 103:8). Once we open our hearts to God, his mercy transforms us, obliterates our sins, fills us with the Holy Spirit and makes us holy in God's presence. His mercy becomes our merit. We thank God for his great mercy in Mass when we say, after the consecration, "We offer you Lord the Bread of life and the Chalice of salvation, giving thanks that you have held us worthy to be in your presence and minister to you."[4] At this moment in the Mass we are accepting ourselves as we truly are in God's presence. We are living by God's word of mercy and love. But why does God love us as he does? How does he really see us? We don't have to guess the answer because God has told us throughout the Scriptures how he sees us. Just consider these words that God speaks to us about ourselves:

We are made in the "image and likeness of God" (Genesis 1:26).

We are "fallen children of Adam" but "redeemed in Christ" (Genesis chapter 3 and 2 Corinthians 5:17).

We are "precious in God's eyes" (Isaiah 43:4).

---

4   Eucharistic Prayer 2

We have been made "little less than a god and crowned with glory and splendour" (Psalm 8:6).

Jesus says that we have been "Born again through water and the Spirit" (John 3:6); he says, "I call you friends" (John 15:15); he invites us to "Make your home in me as I make mine in you" (John 15:3).

St Paul assures us that we are "the temple of the Holy Spirit" (1 Corinthians 6:19), "God's work of art" (Ephesians 2:10), "The body of Christ" (1 Corinthians 12:27).

These are most extraordinary words revealing to us how God sees us, how Christ loves to be with us. Summing up what it means to live by God's word Jesus says, "If anyone loves me he will keep my word, and my Father will love him, and we will come to him and make our home with him" (John 14:23). We now have to "keep Christ's word", we have to live by it and we have to see ourselves in its light. Again the Scripture says about God's word, "Your word is a lamp to my feet, a light on my path" (Psalm 119:105). Without the light of God's word we stumble in the darkness; we cannot understand ourselves. Benedict XVI said,

> We were created in the word and we live in the word; we cannot understand ourselves unless we are open to this dialogue. The word of God discloses the filial and relational nature of human existence... In this dialogue with God we come to understand ourselves and we discover an answer to our heart's deepest question.[5]

It is only in the word of God that we find "the answer to our heart's deepest question".[6] That is why Pope Benedict said,

> It is decisive from the pastoral standpoint to present the word of God in its capacity to enter into dialogue with the everyday problems which people face...We need to make

---

5   Benedict XVI, Verbum Domini, 22/23
6   *Ibid*, 23

every effort to share the word of God as an openness to our problems, a response to our questions, a broadening of our values and the fulfilment of our aspirations.[7]

Christ invites us to enter into dialogue with his word, to ponder his word, to believe his word and to build our lives on his word. His word gives us a sure foundation for our lives. He says to us,

Everyone who listens to these words of mine and acts on them will be like a sensible man who built his house on rock. Rain came down, floods rose, gales blew and hurled themselves against that house, and it did not fall: it was founded on rock. But everyone who listens to these words of mine and does not act on them will be like a stupid man who built his house on sand. Rain came down, floods rose, gales blew and struck that house, and it fell; and what a fall it had (Matthew 7:24-27).

Fr Eugene's story

So often good people hear the words that God speaks to them about themselves and deep down they refuse to accept them. When I was in our International Renewal Centre, Hawkstone Hall, I received a phone call one afternoon from a bishop. He asked me if I could help one of his priests. He said he had a big problem but he didn't want to talk about it over the phone. At that time we had a three-month Renewal Course with sixty priests and religious brothers and sisters underway, but we had one room free. I told the bishop that we could accommodate his priest and he said that he would arrive that evening. When I put the phone down, I began to become a little bit concerned. What kind of a problem would this man be bringing into the group? They were in the fourth week of their renewal course and they were well settled in. When the priest, we will call Fr Eugene, arrived I had a first session with him after the evening meal. He told me that his big problem was that he couldn't pray. I have to say that on hearing

---

7   *Ibid* 23

this I heaved a great sigh of relief! I thought I knew something about that kind of struggle. Then he told me his story. Fr Eugene had been fifteen years as a chaplain in the army. When he took up his first appointment as a parish priest he succeeded an old priest who had been in that parish for thirty-five years and during those years, as he said, "the Vatican Council got nowhere near his parish". Now Fr Eugene arrived as an energetic priest in his late forties, full of zeal, doing everything that the Vatican Council encouraged the parish priest to do. The people were loving it, praising him to the sky, but he himself was not praying. He was, of course, saying the official prayers of the Church, but he felt that he had no personal relationship with the Lord. The praise of the people was beginning to get to him. He was feeling a hypocrite. In fact, he was heading for a nervous breakdown. A priest friend in whom he confided encouraged him to take time away. So here he was in our Centre looking for help. When I heard his story I opened chapter 43 of Isaiah and asked him to read it out loud to me. He was slightly taken aback, but he began reading the familiar passage:

> Do not be afraid, for I have redeemed you;
> I have called you by your name, you are mine.
> Should you pass through the sea, I will be with you;
> or through rivers, they will not swallow you up…
> I give Egypt for your ransom,
> and exchange Cush and Seba for you.
> Because you are precious in my eyes,
> because you are honoured and I love you (Isaiah 43:2. 4).

I stopped him when he read those words "you are precious in my eyes" and I asked him to respond to God. He pondered in silence for a while and then he banged the table at me and said very forcefully, "He is not speaking to me." He believed every one of his parishioners was precious in God's eyes but he couldn't believe it of himself. That was his problem with prayer. He felt, deep down in his religious consciousness, that God just about tolerated him but didn't really think much of him. So, he was keeping out of God's sight as much as he could! When we discussed this at some length I invited him to come down with me to the Holy Hour and to sit before the Blessed Sacrament and just say, "Jesus I thank you that I am precious in your Father's eyes." He said he would give it a try. And he did. Each evening he was there at the Holy Hour. After about three days, Fr Eugene was so full of prayer, he couldn't stop praying. He was spending hours in the church. What had happened? He had begun to live by the word of God. In the depth of his heart he accepted himself as precious in God's eyes. He discovered his true self and began to live a life of self-acceptance rather than of self-rejection. He accepted that the mercy of God is his merit. He developed true self-esteem. Now he could come with joy into the presence of God and talk with him. That is the transforming power of living by the word of God. Fr Eugene refused to live any longer by someone's destructive word or by the negative, critical word that he so often spoke to himself about himself. He silenced that inner critic that is in all of us.

True self-esteem

After a month of prayer and study he left our Centre and went back to his parish in a joyful spirit and with true self-esteem. Richard Gula gives us this helpful definition of self-esteem:

> Self-esteem is the virtue by which we accept ourselves as being worthwhile apart from our achievements... God's love bestows our worth. The act of faith on our part is to believe that to be true, to accept that we have been accepted and to claim our worth. That may be our most difficult act of faith, but it is foundational to self-esteem.[8]

When Fr Eugene arrived at our Centre he couldn't "accept that he had been accepted", he could not accept that he was precious in God's

---

8   Richard Gula, *Just Ministry*, (New York: Paulist Press, 2010), 90

eyes. That was why he had such a struggle with personal prayer and why he was feeling depressed and defeated. The transforming grace of living by God's word that he was precious in God's eyes, that God's mercy was his merit, freed him for a zealous life of evangelisation. Pope Francis could have had him in mind when he wrote,

> May the world of our time, which is searching, sometimes with anguish, sometimes with hope, be enabled to receive the good news not from evangelisers who are dejected, discouraged, impatient or anxious, but from ministers of the Gospel whose lives glow with fervour, who have first received the joy of Christ.[9]

Fr Eugene had received "the joy of Christ" not by study, nor by listening to theological lectures, but by silently sitting in the presence of the Blessed Sacrament and saying that little prayer, "Jesus I thank you that I am precious in your Father's sight". As he renewed his faith in this word of God he began to do what Jesus asks us to do, namely "to live by every word that comes from the mouth of God". Living by the word of God is not just thinking about it or meditating on it, good as these activities are, but "putting the word into practice". When the woman in the Gospel said to Jesus, "Happy the womb that bore you and the breast you sucked", Jesus replied, "Still happier those who hear the word of God and keep it" or, as some translations prefer, "Happy rather those who hear God's word and put it into practice" (Luke 11: 28). The word of God, if we keep it faithfully or if we act on it, brings the blessing of happiness into our lives.

Fr Eugene experienced the blessing of happiness because he discovered the love of God in an altogether new way by coming to realise that God's love is his mercy. The words of the psalm spoke clearly to him: "Indeed how good is the Lord, eternal his merciful love" (Psalm 100). God's love is God's mercy. When St Paul says, "The love of God has been poured into our hearts by the

---

9   Pope Francis, *The Joy of the Gospel*, 10

Holy Spirit which has been given to us" (Romans 5:5), he is also saying the mercy of God has been poured into our hearts through the Holy Spirit who has been given to us. It is that gift of merciful love poured into our hearts by the Holy Spirit which assures us that we are the children of God. As St Paul says, "The proof that you are sons is that God has sent the Spirit of his Son into our hearts: the Spirit that cries, 'Abba, Father', and it is this that makes you a son, you are not a slave any more" (Galatians 4:6). That was the great enlightenment that Fr Eugene received. Theoretically, of course, he knew that he was a son of God. He could even preach good sermons on God's love to his parishioners. But theoretical knowledge of his faith didn't touch his heart. Benedict XVI could have been describing Fr Eugene's condition when he asked this question:

> Can our encounter with the God who, in Christ, has shown us his face and opened his heart, be for us too not just "informative" but "performative" – that is to say, can it change our lives, so that we know we are redeemed through the hope that it expresses?[10]

God's word had become performative, indeed we can say it had become transformative, in Fr Eugene's life. Now he gratefully accepted that he was a son of the Father, not a slave; he accepted himself as a friend of Jesus, not a bonded servant; he truly believed that he was the temple of the Holy Spirit, filled and renewed with the mercy of God.

The neglect of mercy in theology

Cardinal Walter Kasper, the great theologian of Mercy, writes, "God's being is revealed in his mercy. Mercy is the expression of the divine essence."[11] When we come into the presence of God we are in the presence of infinite mercy. When Eugene sat before the Blessed Sacrament he was in the presence of mercy incarnate.

---

10 Pope Benedict XVI, Spe Salvi: On Christian Hope, 4
11 Cardinal Walter Kasper, *Mercy: The Essence of the Gospel and the Key to Christian Life*, Paulist Press, New York, 2014, p.51

Jesus is the very incarnation of divine mercy. As Pope Francis says, "Jesus Christ is the face of the Father's mercy"[12]. As Fr Eugene contemplated the face of Jesus in the Blessed Sacrament he was seeing and experiencing the mercy of God the Father. Yet, Fr Eugene's theology at that time had very little to say to him about mercy. Kasper points out that mercy, this very "expression of the divine essence", has been glaringly neglected in dogmatic theology. He writes, under the heading:

> Mercy: Criminally Neglected
> Emphasising mercy as the central topic for theology means to pursue anew the central meaning of the message of divine mercy in the testimony of the Old as well as the New Testament. As soon as one tries to do this, we make the astounding, in fact shocking, realisation that this topic, which is so central for the Bible and so relevant for the present experience of reality, appears at best in the margins of the lexica and handbooks of dogmatic theology. In the traditional as well as in the more recent dogmatic handbooks, God's mercy is treated only as one of God's attributes among others. Most often it is treated only briefly and then only after the attributes that derive from God's metaphysical essence… In the more recent handbooks, mercy is often completely absent… Exceptions prove the rule; they cannot, however, fundamentally change this general finding.[13]

Kasper also draws attention to the fact that he himself didn't give mercy its proper place in his earlier writings: "I overlooked and passed over the idea of mercy in my exposition of the doctrine of God in *The God of Jesus Christ*."[14] No wonder, therefore, that so many good people, like Fr Eugene, struggle with intimacy with God in prayer. If mercy is not at the forefront of their thinking about God, if they have not been taught to see in Jesus Christ the face of the Father's mercy, their relationship with God will be dominated

---

12 Pope Francis, Bull of Indiction of the Extraordinary Jubilee Year of Mercy, 1
13 *Ibid*, 10-11
14 *Ibid*, chapter 1, endnote 36

by fear. Because they believe in the all holy God, who detests sin, they unconsciously begin to think that because they have sinned God really detests them. They despair of holiness. This is a direct contradiction of God's word: "Yet you are merciful to all, because you can do all things and overlook men's sins so that they can repent. Yes, you love all that exists, you hold nothing of what you have made in abhorrence, for had you hated anything, you would not have formed it" (Wisdom 11:23-25).

Pope Francis has this liberating word of encouragement for all of us:

> To become a saint only one thing is necessary; to accept the grace which the Father gives us in Jesus Christ. This grace changes our heart. We continue to be sinners for we are weak, but with this grace which makes us feel that the Lord is good, that the Lord is merciful, that the Lord waits for us, that the Lord pardons us, that this immense grace changes our heart.[15]

God of mercy

God revealed himself as the God of mercy. Moses, having led God's people out of slavery in Egypt into freedom, pleaded with God to let him see his glory. And God said to him: "I will let all my splendour pass in front of you, and I will pronounce before you the name Yahweh (Lord). I have compassion on whom I will, and I show pity to whom I please" (Exodus 33:19). Then, in a wonderful revelation of his glory on Mount Sinai, the Lord came down to be with Moses. We read, "The Lord descended in the form of a cloud, and Moses stood with him there. He called on the name of the Lord. The Lord passed before him and proclaimed, 'The Lord, the Lord, a God of tenderness and compassion, slow to anger, rich in kindness and faithfulness; for thousands he maintains his kindness, forgives faults, transgressions, sin; yet he lets nothing go unchecked'" (Exodus 34:5-7).

---

15 Pope Francis, *The Church of Mercy*, Darton, Longman and Todd, London 2014, p. 14

God reveals his innermost nature as mercy, compassion, faithfulness and tender love for his people. And even when his people turned their backs on him and served false gods, God remained true to himself and refused to take revenge on them. He revealed his heart for his people:

> My heart recoils from it
> My whole being trembles at the thought
> I will not give rein to my fierce anger.
> I will not destroy Ephraim again,
> For I am God, not man;
> I am the Holy One in your midst
> And have no wish to destroy (Hosea 11:9).

The God of mercy is always faithful to his mercy. He is always true to himself. In the words of the Blessed Virgin Mary, God has come "to the help of Israel his servant, mindful of his mercy... of his mercy to Abraham and his descendants for ever" (Luke 1:54-55). She also said God's mercy is inexhaustible because "his mercy reaches from age to age for those who fear him" (Luke1:50). Our Lady explained to her cousin Elizabeth that the momentous event of her having conceived the Word of God in her womb, through the power of the Holy Spirit, was the act of God remembering his mercy. Her pregnancy was a manifestation of the mercy of the Father. That is why we see in Jesus the face of the Father's mercy and why the proclamation that Jesus Christ is our Redeemer must always be the proclamation of mercy. As Pope Francis says:

> The time has come for the Church to take up the joyful call to mercy once more. It is time to return to the basics and to bear the weaknesses and the struggles of our brothers and sisters. Mercy is the force that reawakens us to new life and instils in us the courage to look to the future with hope.[16]

---

16 Pope Francis, Misericordiae Vultus: Bull of Indiction of the Extraordinary Jubilee of Mercy, 10

Personal spiritual exercise

Centre yourself; sitting upright; breathing rhythmically; clearing your mind of all preoccupations.

Bring yourself to bodily stillness.

Now calmly say to yourself: "The mercy of God is my merit."

Repeat this phrase to yourself a few times and absorb its meaning.

Now be still in the presence of the God of mercy and compassion.

Now focus again on your breathing as you relax in God's presence.

And bring yourself gently back to the world.

This spiritual exercise will deepen your awareness of being in the presence of the God of mercy and open your heart to receive unconditionally the blessing of mercy.

— Chapter Two —

A drama of divine mercy

Jesus, we are told, came bringing "the Good News from God" (Mark 1:15). He had extraordinary good news for the people of his home town of Nazareth and for all the people of Israel. But right from the start of his preaching and teaching he encountered opposition. His fellow citizens in Nazareth were perplexed by the sudden and unexpected emergence in Jesus of a wisdom and a power they never suspected. They thought they knew him well. He grew up with them and he was one of them. When he began to teach them in their synagogue they were amazed at his message and at his skills in delivering it and the miracles that were happening at his word. They began to ask themselves:

> "Where did the man get all this? What is this wisdom that has been granted him, and these miracles that are worked through him? This is the carpenter, surely, the son of Mary, the brother of James and Joset and Jude and Simon. His sisters, too, are they not here with us?" And they would not accept him (Mark 6: 2-4).

The scribes and Pharisees, the religious elite of Israel, were not prepared to listen to him either because they knew that he had not attended a rabbinic school nor sat at the feet of a great teacher of the Law like Nicodemus or Gamaliel, and therefore he had nothing to teach them. It was their right to teach him and his duty to learn from them and obey them.

Jesus' parables reveal God's mercy

With great compassion in his heart for the closed-mindedness of his fellow citizens in Nazareth and for the spiritual blindness of the religious leaders of the people, Jesus devised a superb method for communicating "the Good News from God". He told the people stories, which we call parables, and through the parables challenged people to take a second look at their deepest convictions about themselves, about their relationship with one another and about their relationship with God. St Luke introduces Jesus' most memorable and best known parable with these words: "The tax collectors and the sinners meanwhile were all seeking his company to hear what he had to say, and the Pharisees and the scribes complained, 'This man' they said, 'welcomes sinners and eats with them'" (Luke 15:1-3). How can Jesus bring "Good News from God" to these critics and invite them to look again at how they see God? Luke says simply "So he spoke this parable to them." In fact, into their very confused way of seeing who God is or how God relates to those whom they call sinners, Jesus spoke three parables. He told the story of a man who had lost a sheep, of the woman who had lost a coin, and then, his best known parable, the story of the man who had lost his son. The first parable is about the farmer who had a hundred sheep and who had lost one. What did he do? He left "the ninety-nine in the wilderness" (Luke 15:4) and went searching for the lost one. And when he found it "he joyfully took it on his shoulders" (Luke 15:5) and carried it back to his farm. And then what did he do? "He called together his friends and neighbours and said, "Rejoice with me... I have found my sheep that was lost." Jesus then drew from the parable this Good News from God: "In the same way, I tell you, there will be more rejoicing in heaven over one repentant sinner than over the ninety-nine virtuous men who have no need of repentance" (Luke 15:7). We can imagine Jesus having a wry smile on his face as he said that, knowing so well that everyone needs repentance. But Jesus makes it very clear that God's ways are not our ways. God doesn't see the world as we see it. God has an eye for the unique value of each individual, even the one whom the scribes and Pharisees may reject as a renegade sinner.

In the second parable, Jesus tells them the story of the woman who had lost a coin: "What woman with ten drachmas would not, if she lost one, light a lamp and sweep out the house and search thoroughly till she found it? And then, when she had found it, call together her friends and neighbours? 'Rejoice with me', she would say, 'I have found the drachma I lost.'" And Jesus draws this conclusion, "In the same way, I tell you, there is rejoicing among the angels of God over one repentant sinner" (Luke 15:8-10). Nothing gives more joy to God than the repentance of the sinner because then God does what only he can do. He receives the sinner into his mercy.

How are we to understand God's act of forgiving, God's exercise of his mercy? In his third parable, in response to the scornful criticism that he "welcomes sinners and eats with them", Jesus told them the story of the father who had lost his "prodigal son", which is the best known of all his parables:

> A man had two sons. The younger said to his father, "Father, let me have the share of the estate that would come to me". So the father divided the property between them. A few days later, the younger got together everything he had and left for a distant country where he squandered his money on a life of debauchery (Luke 15:11-13).

A dramatic opening

This is the most dramatic opening to any of Jesus' parables. It has implications for all the family. And, as Fr Denis McBride observes:

> None of the family emerges unscathed from this opening scene. The son requests a portion of the substance (ousia) and the narrator remarks that the son's selfish request leads the father to give away not just his livelihood but his life. In agreeing without protest to this, the father jeopardises the

family honour in the eyes of others. And in not protesting about what is happening, but in receiving, instead, his own share of the property, the elder brother is culpable of standing by while the family breaks up.[1]

How is the story of that young man going to end? We can imagine those Pharisees, to whom Jesus was telling this story, being filled with righteous indignation. And they are not surprised when the next scene describes how the young man runs out of money and meets with disaster. We read:

> When he had spent all his money, that country experienced a severe famine, and now he began to feel the pinch, so he hired himself out to one of the local inhabitants who put him on his farm to feed the pigs. And he would willingly have filled his belly with the husks the pigs were eating but no one offered him anything (Luke 15:14-16).

Down in the gutter

Nothing more degrading could happen to a young Jewish man. He had lost, not just his inheritance, he had lost his dignity as well. Pigs were unclean animals and there he was mixing with them and feeding them and even longing to eat their very food. The prodigal's dream for a world of unrestrained freedom and pleasure in "a distant country" had now become his nightmare existence as a swineherd. How is he going to survive? The story begins to take an inward journey:

> Then he came to his senses and said, "How many of my father's paid servants have more food than they want, and here am I dying of hunger! I will leave this place and go to my father and say: Father, I have sinned against heaven and against you; I no longer deserve to be called your son; treat me as one of your paid servants." So he left the place and went back to his father (Luke 15:17-20).

---

1   Denis McBride C.Ss.R., *The Parables of Jesus*, Redemptorist Publications, Chawton, Hampshire 1999, p.139

The young spendthrift "came to his senses". Benedict XVI points out that a better translation is "he went into himself".[2] In journeying to "the distant country" he was really distancing himself from his true self, from his true homeland. He begins to remember that he once had a different life when he was at home in his father's house. He is getting in touch with the dignity that he believes he has lost forever by turning his back on God and on his father and living a life of debauchery. Benedict XVI wrote:

> He is on a pilgrimage toward the truth of his existence, and that means "homeward". When the Church Fathers offer this "existential" exposition of the son's journey home, they are also explaining to us what "conversion" is, what sort of sufferings and inner purifications it involves, and we may safely say that they understood the essence of the parable correctly and help us to realise its relevance for today.[3]

The prodigal's self-esteem is at rock bottom. Gone is the false self-assurance he had when he demanded his share of the estate. He will be happy if he can begin again, not as a son, but as a paid servant. He will confess his sins to his father, acknowledge that he no longer deserves to be called his son and take on a new identity as servant in his father's house. As St John Paul II observed:

> He realises that he no longer has any right except to be an employee in his father's house. His decision is taken in full consciousness of what he has deserved and of what he can still have a right to in accordance with the norms of justice. Precisely this reasoning demonstrates that, at the centre of the prodigal's consciousness, the sense of lost dignity is emerging, the sense of that dignity that springs from the relationship of the son with the father. And it is with this decision that he sets out.[4]

---

2   Benedict XVI, *Jesus of Nazareth*, vol. 1, Bloomsbury, London 2007, p.204

3   *Ibid* 205

4   St John Paul II, *On the Mercy of God*, 1980, para 5

As Jesus prepares his audience for the return of the son to the father's house, all eyes will be fixed on the father. How will he react when the son walks in to make his confession and look for a paid job? Will he keep him outside the door or will he invite him in? The father does neither. Jesus tells us what the father does in these words:

> While he was still a long way off, his father saw him and was moved with pity. He ran to the boy, clasped him in his arms and kissed him tenderly. Then his son said, "Father, I have sinned against heaven and against you. I no longer deserve to be called your son." But the father said to his servants, "Quick! Bring out the best robe and put it on him; put a ring on his finger and scandals on his feet. Bring the calf we have been fattening, and kill it; we are going to have a feast, a celebration, because this son of mine was dead and has come back to life; he was lost and is found." And they began to celebrate (Luke 15:21-24).

What a dramatisation of mercy! Jesus told the parable in response to the Pharisees' criticism of him "welcoming sinners and eating with them" (Luke 15:3). Now those same Pharisees will have to judge the actions of the father. The prodigal felt that he had no right to be called the father's son and the Pharisees would surely agree with that. But the father was fully aware that he had a right and a duty to be his son's father. And that surely challenges the Pharisees. The son's sins certainly hurt the father, but beneath those sins the father sees the dignity and worth of his destitute son who is trying to find his way back to his father's house. The father is also aware that when the son departed from him, for the freedom of a distant land, he didn't cease to be his father and he didn't depart from his son. He had watched every day for his son's return. That is why he was able to see him "while he was still a long way off". As Pope Francis writes:

The son was always in the father's heart, even though he had left him, even though he had squandered his whole inheritance, his freedom. The Father, with patience, love, hope and mercy had never for a second stopped thinking about him, and as soon as he sees him still far off, he runs out to meet him and embrace him with tenderness, the tenderness of God, without a word of reproach: he has returned. And that is the joy of the Father... God is always waiting for us and never grows tired.[5]

Love is transformed into mercy

The father could never abandon his own son. He would always be his son. The son believed that that there was no way back for him into the bosom of his family. He believed that his sins had robbed him of his rights as a son. But, while the father had "lost his son", the son had never lost his father. Now, by his dramatic manifestation of his love, the father begins to heal that famine of love in his son's heart which robbed him of the sense of his dignity and worth as a human being and as the son of his father.

The father's right to be faithful to his paternal love for his son is manifested in his merciful welcome-home embrace, without judgement or demand for justice and restitution. There is no mention of either justice or restitution in the parable. St John Paul II writes:

> Nevertheless, the relationship between justice and love that is manifested as mercy, is inscribed with great exactness in the Gospel parable. It becomes more evident that love is transformed into mercy when it is necessary to go beyond the precise norm of justice – precise and often narrow.[6]

Love is transformed into mercy! The father's love for his prodigal son knows no bounds. He commands his servants to serve his son, to respect him, to treat him with dignity and not to scorn him because of

---

5   Pope Francis, *The Church of Mercy*, Darton, Longman and Todd, London 2014, 3
6   St John Paul II, *On the Mercy of God*, 1980, para 5

the disgrace he had brought upon the family. So, the servants clothe the returning prodigal with the best robe: the sign of his restored dignity as son; they put a ring on his finger: the sign of his restored authority as son; and they put sandals on his feet: the sign that he is not a slave any more. And then the father calls for a celebration, a big feast, because "this son of mine was dead and has come back to life; he was lost and is found". And they began to celebrate (Luke 15:24).

The joy that the father experiences in his son's return has to be expressed in a welcome-home feast to which all are invited. Denis McBride points out that:

> The killing of the fatted calf – rather than a sheep or goat – is an indication that the village would be invited to join in the feast. As K.E. Bailey observes: "To kill a calf and not invite the community would be an insult to the community and a waste for the family". Indeed, the main point of killing such a large animal is to be able to invite the entire community. As with the woman and the shepherd, the joy must be shared on all sides.[7]

The outsider

Just before he told this parable Jesus said, "I tell you, there will be more rejoicing in heaven over one repentant sinner than over ninety-nine virtuous men who have no need of repentance" (Luke 15:7). Now the father and his reconciled son and the servants and the villagers join in celebrating the father's joy at the safe return of his son. But there is one man who will have nothing to do with the celebration. That is the eldest son, the prodigal's brother. He remains outside and refuses to join the celebration. This is how the Gospel begins to tell his story:

> Now the elder son was out in the fields, and on his way back, as he drew near the house, he could hear music and dancing. Calling one of the servants he asked what it was

---

7   *Ibid.* p.143

all about. "Your brother has come" replied the servant "and your father has killed the calf we had fattened because he has got him back safe and sound". He was angry then and refused to go in (Luke 15:25-27).

The joy of the father is once again turned to sadness by a son. How could his elder son not share in his joy at the safe return of his younger brother? So the father goes out to plead with his elder son.

But he answered his father, "Look, all these years I have slaved for you and never once disobeyed your orders, yet you never offered me so much as a kid for me to celebrate with my friends. But, for this son of yours, when he comes back after swallowing up your property – he and his women – you kill the calf we have been fattening" (Luke 15:29-30).

It is a devastating attack that left the father bewildered. He can only reply with a re-assuring gentleness and love:

"My son, you are with me always and all I have is yours. But it was only right we should celebrate and rejoice, because your brother here was dead and has come to life; he was lost and is found" (Luke 15:31-32).

Who is the father in the parable?

As we reflect on this parable it is helpful to ask ourselves these questions: Who is the father in the parable? Who is the youngest son, the prodigal? Who is the elder brother? St John Paul II answers the first question in this way:

There is no doubt that in this simple and penetrating analogy the figure of the father reveals God as Father... The father of the prodigal son is faithful to his fatherhood, faithful to the love that he always lavished on his son.[8]

---

8   St John Paul II, *On the Mercy of God*, 1980, para 5

The father's faithful love, his fidelity to his fatherhood, becomes mercy for his son who "was dead and who has come to life". Notice what love as mercy seeks. It seeks to secure the restoration of the dignity of the prodigal, the reawakening in the prodigal of the sense of his own worth as a person and the enhancement of true self-esteem as being son of the father. The father said of his prodigal son, "he was lost and now he is found". The prodigal, in his turn, must make that same discovery. He must be able to say, with deep conviction, "I had lost my true self and now I have found my true self again. And my true self assures me that I am the son of my father." If the father counts him worthy to be his son then he is truly his son. We acknowledge that God the Father counts us worthy at Mass when we say, after the Consecration, "You have held us worthy to be in your presence and minister to you".[9]

Who is the prodigal?

The critics who fail to see that love is at the heart of mercy, and that mercy is a response to the goodness in the heart of the human being, no matter how "lost" the person may have become by living an evil or debauched life, often complain that showing mercy demeans the person, just turning him or her into an object of cold pity. The truth is the exact opposite. Mercy discovers the buried worth of the person: "my son was dead and has come to life." As Cardinal Schoenborn writes:

> Mercy means not devaluing the other but rather seeing him in his dignity and thereby helping him to stand upright. This is precisely what makes it possible for the prodigal son to see himself and his deeds in the fullness of truth. Only in the light of this complete acceptance does it become possible to look at one's own misery, failure, and the burden of having lost one's gifts without being overwhelmed by it. In this way one can acknowledge one's failure and need not repress it.[10]

---

9   Eucharistic prayer 2
10 Christoph Cardinal Schoenborn, *We Have Found Mercy: The Mystery of God's Merciful Love,* Ignatius Press, San Francisco, 2012, p.20

The prodigal's experience of receiving mercy, that is, the loving kindness and acceptance of his father, liberates him from the prison of his own self rejection and self-condemnation and enables him to receive once again his birthright as son. Each of us who repents our sins is the prodigal. We are saying, with the prodigal, "I will arise and go to my Father." And when we come to the Father, we receive the same welcome home as the prodigal received. Jesus says that "there is rejoicing among the angels of God over one repentant sinner" (Luke 15:8-10). Our repentance, whatever the sin, gives joy to heaven. The merciful father in the parable is greatly enriched through his gift of mercy because now he can say "my son was lost and is found". His son was of much greater value to him than all the property he had squandered. While the prodigal is blessed by receiving his father's merciful embrace the father himself is blessed and comforted in giving that embrace. As Shakespeare said,

> The quality of mercy is not strained;
> It droppeth as the gentle rain from heaven
> Upon the place beneath. It is twice blessed.
> It blesseth him that gives and him that takes.[11]

Who is the elder son?

The Pharisees, who had been complaining about Jesus "welcoming sinners and eating with them", would be feeling a lot of sympathy for the elder son. He was their kind of man. He had stayed at home with his father, worked hard all his life and "never once disobeyed his orders". And what reward did he get? He said, "You never offered me so much as a kid for me to celebrate with my friends." Deep down, despite all his outward fidelity, he was clearly feeling bitter against his father. Although he had "the freedom of his father's house", that freedom had turned into slavery. While "never once disobeying" he resented his father's authority. His service had become a drudgery rather than a gift of love in response to the father's love. The father's loving mercy for his younger brother touches something very raw

---

11 Merchant of Venice, Act 4, Scene 1

within him. Long repressed bitterness and resentments erupt when he hears the music and the dancing and is told that his father has invited the whole village to a feast to celebrate his brother's return. Sadly there are always people with the elder son's attitude in our Church today, people who can say to God, "I never once disobeyed you" and use their external obedience to justify their sitting in judgement on other people. While examining this religious frame of mind, Benedict XV1 proposes the remedy:

> For them, more than anything else, God is Law; they see themselves in a juridical relationship with God and in that relationship they are at rights with him. But God is greater. They need to convert from the Law-God to the greater God, the God of love. This will not mean giving up their obedience, but rather that this obedience will flow from deeper wellsprings, and will therefore be bigger, more open and purer, but above all more humble.[12]

There can be a "bit of the elder son" in all of us. We have to remind ourselves every day that we are sinners who have been reconciled with God, not because we have done all he has asked us to do, but because he has loved us "with an everlasting love" (Jeremiah 31:3). God hates sin but loves the sinner. Beneath the sin God sees the person made in his own image and likeness, the person whom he loves with an everlasting love. God speaks his word of mercy and forgiveness into our hearts that calls us to return to our Father's house. The Father welcomes even the greatest sinners and celebrates their return. If we don't want to be like the elder brother in the parable we must join in the celebration and give praise to the Father for his great mercy.

---

12 Benedict XVI, *Jesus of Nazareth*, vol. 1, Bloomsbury, London 2007, p.211

Every time we celebrate Mass, each of us publicly confesses to God and to one another that we have greatly sinned in what we have done and in what we have failed to do, and we emphasise this fact with the words "through my fault, through my most grievous fault". We identify with the prodigal and not with the elder brother. When we hear the call to repent our sins we have the grace to return to the Father and the "inheritance of our heart", which we have received from the Father, becomes alive and active in our hearts. As St John Paul II wrote:

> Called in that truth which has been his inheritance "of the beginning", the inheritance of his heart, which is deeper than the sinfulness inherited... Christ's words, set in the whole reality of creation and redemption, re-activate that deepest inheritance and give it real power in human life.[13]

The prodigal had lost the material inheritance that he had received from his father. His elder brother bitterly reminded his father of this fact when he refused to join the celebration that his father had arranged for his prodigal son's return: "When he comes back after swallowing up your property – he and his women – you kill the calf we have been fattening" (Luke 15:29-30). But in the father's eyes the "inheritance of the heart" that his son had received from him cannot be compared to the property he had given him. And now he celebrates because that "deepest inheritance of the heart has been activated". His son has been restored to his full dignity as his father's son. Conversion happens when that "inheritance of the heart" is activated by the word of God.

We, as sinners, always receive from God the welcome-home embrace that the prodigal son received from his father on his return home. Cardinal Kasper applies the parable to each of us personally and he writes:

---

13 St John Paul II, *The Theology of the Body*, 46: 6, Pauline Press, Boston 2006

Jesus wants to say to us: your story is told in the story of the prodigal son. You yourself are the prodigal son; you too must repent. But have no fear. God himself comes to meet you and takes you in his arms. He does not humiliate you, rather, he gives you back your dignity as a son.[14]

The parable of the prodigal expresses Jesus' teaching on God's mercy in the fullest way possible. The Father remains the Father and the son remains his son. The Father rushing to embrace the son is being true to himself and is thereby restoring the son's dignity and place in the family. The Father of mercy rushes to meet us every time we turn to him for mercy. There is joy in heaven, Jesus assures us, when we acknowledge our sins and ask for forgiveness. We pray never to fall into the slavery of the elder son. God never humiliates us. He defends and restores our dignity as his sons and daughters. As St John Paul II said, "The relationship of mercy is based on the common experience of that good which is man, on the common experience of the dignity that is proper to him".[15]

Personal spiritual exercise

Centre yourself; sitting upright; breathing rhythmically; clearing your mind of all preoccupations.

Bring yourself to bodily stillness.

Now calmly acknowledge that you are the prodigal in the parable.

Experience the Father rushing to embrace you and welcome you.

Be still for some time in the presence of the God of mercy and compassion and receive his love.

Now focus again on your breathing as you relax in God's presence.

And bring yourself gently back to the world.

---

14 Cardinal Walter Kasper, *Mercy: The Essence of the Gospel and the Key to Christian Life*, Paulist Press, New York, 2014, p.72
15 St John Paul II, *Mercy*, 6

This spiritual exercise will deepen your awareness of being in the presence of the God of mercy and show you how God has embraced you with his love and mercy.

— Chapter Three —

Mercy has been shown to me

Nothing illustrates more clearly the transforming power of God's mercy than the life of Saul of Tarsus, whom we know and revere as St Paul the Apostle. Saul was a devout Jew, a Pharisee of the strictest observance. When the first Christian, St Stephen, was being stoned to death, because of his witness to the resurrection of Jesus Christ, those who were stoning Stephen "put down their clothes at the feet of a young man called Saul... Saul entirely approved of the killing" (Acts of the Apostles 7:59-60). After that first 'taste of blood' Saul embarked on his own crusade against the disciples of Jesus. We read, "Saul then worked for the total destruction of the Church; he went from house to house arresting both men and women and sending them to prison" (Acts 8:3). He didn't limit his attack on the small Christian community to the city of Jerusalem where the Church of Christ first appeared. Christians had to be eliminated wherever they were. As Acts records, "Saul was still breathing threats to slaughter the Lord's disciples. He had gone to the high priest and asked for letters addressed to the synagogues in Damascus, that would authorise him to arrest and take to Jerusalem any followers of the Way, men or women that he could find" (Acts of the Apostles 9:1-2). Writing to the Philippians years later Paul reminded them, "I was a persecutor of the Church" (Philippians 3:6).

How could a man, filled with such persecuting zeal, a man who rejoiced even in the death of St Stephen and in the imprisonment of men and women for their faith in Jesus, become the great apostle St Paul? Writing from his prison cell, towards the end of his life, to his disciple and helper Timothy, Paul said,

I used to be a blasphemer and did all I could to injure and discredit the faith. Mercy, however, was shown me, because until I became a believer I had been acting in ignorance; and the grace of our Lord filled me with faith and with the love that is in Christ Jesus. Here is a saying that you can rely on and nobody should doubt: that Christ Jesus came into the world to save sinners. I myself am the greatest of them; and if mercy has been shown to me, it is because Jesus Christ meant to make me the greatest evidence of his inexhaustible patience for all the other people who would later have to trust in him to come to eternal life (1 Timothy1:13-16).

Paul says that "the mercy shown to him" brought about that amazing spiritual transformation that changed him from being Saul, the persecutor of all Christians, to being St Paul, the Apostle of the Gentiles. And how was that mercy shown to him?

St Paul's story

Paul recounts the story of how he was embraced with mercy on three separate occasions. It was an encounter with the person of Jesus Christ. He was on his way to the city of Damascus, armed with the authority of the High Priest in Jerusalem, to arrest the Christians he found there and bring them back to Jerusalem to face trial. This is how the first account of his conversion is recorded:

Suddenly, while he was travelling to Damascus and just before he reached the city, there came a light from heaven all round him. He fell to the ground, and then he heard a voice saying, "Saul, Saul, why are you persecuting me?" "Who are you, Lord?" he asked, and the voice answered, "I am Jesus, and you are persecuting me. Get up now and go into the city, and you will be told what you have to do." The men travelling with Saul stood there speechless, for though they heard the voice they could see no one. Saul got up from the ground, but even with his eyes wide open he could see nothing at all, and they had to lead him into Damascus by the hand. For three days he was without his sight, and took neither food nor drink (Acts 9:3-9).

For three full days Saul found himself in a place of darkness, remembering, no doubt, that great light and the voice that identified himself as "I am Jesus and you are persecuting me". He would also have been pondering what the voice said, "go into the city and you will be told what you have to do". Who is going to tell him? He had to wait. The person who was going to tell him was being prepared for this work. The account in Acts continues:

> A disciple called Ananias who lived in Damascus had a vision in which he heard the Lord say to him, "Ananias!" When he replied, "Here I am, Lord", the Lord said, "You must go to Straight Street and ask at the house of Judas for someone called Saul, who comes from Tarsus. At this moment he is praying, having had a vision of a man called Ananias coming in and laying hands on him to give him back his sight" (Acts 9:10-12).

It was to arrest people like Ananias that Saul had embarked on his journey to Damascus in the first place. Ananias is on such familiar terms with the Lord that he feels free to draw this to his attention! He said,

> "Lord, several people have told me about this man and all the harm he has been doing to your saints in Jerusalem. He has only come here because he holds a warrant from the chief priests to arrest everybody who invokes your name". The Lord replied, "You must go all the same, because this man is my chosen instrument to bring my name before pagans and pagan kings and before the people of Israel"... Then Ananias went. He entered the house, and at once laid

his hands on Saul and said, "Brother Saul, I have been sent by the Lord Jesus who appeared to you on your way here so that you may recover your sight and be filled with the Holy Spirit". Immediately it was as though scales fell away from Saul's eyes, and he could see again. So he was baptised there and then, and after taking some food he regained his strength (Acts 9:13-19).

Paul could never forget this transforming grace of mercy that had enveloped and renewed his whole being and how, through the ministry of the Church in Damascus, through Ananias, he was "born again through water and the Spirit" (John 3:5). Jesus, who had appeared to him on the road, had sent him to his Church in Damascus, the Church which Paul immediately recognised as the "body of Christ". He saw in the amazing mercy shown to him the clearest possible evidence that God wills the salvation of every human being and that if such mercy had been granted to him, who was the greatest sinner, then no one should ever despair of receiving God's mercy. As he wrote to Timothy, "Jesus Christ meant to make me the greatest evidence of his inexhaustible patience for all other people who would later have to trust in him to come to eternal life" (I Timothy 1:16). The very murderous, persecuting zeal of Saul was the clearest evidence of the mercy of God, the mercy that changed Saul into Paul.

St Paul, the evangelist of mercy

St Paul, through his own experience of the transforming power of God's mercy, became the great evangelist of mercy. Paul's witness to mercy still says to each of us today, "If such great mercy was shown to me, the greatest sinner, why would you doubt that mercy will be shown to you too?" And Paul gives us the fundamental reason why he can be so certain of this:

What proves that God loves us is that Christ died for us while we were still sinners. Having died to make us righteous, is it likely that he would now fail to save us from God's anger? When we were reconciled to God by the death of his Son, we were still enemies; now that we have been reconciled, surely we may count on being saved by the life of his Son? Not merely because we have been reconciled but because we are filled with joyful trust in God, through our Lord Jesus Christ, through whom we have already gained our reconciliation (Romans 5:8-11).

Paul knew, of course, that his new vision of a God who loves sinners, and whom, from now on, he will call "the Father of mercies and the God of all consolation" (2 Corinthians 1:2), can be known only through the revelation of Jesus Christ. And Jesus gave us that revelation, not in words only, but by what he did for us: "Christ died for us while we were still sinners." Jesus didn't die on the cross because we are saints already. He died on the cross because we are called and destined to be saints. As Jesus said to Nicodemus, "God loved the world so much that he gave his only Son, so that everyone who believes in him may not be lost but may have eternal life. For God sent his Son into the world, not to condemn the world, but so that through him the world might be saved" (John 3:16-17). Paul has now experienced in his own life the full reality of what Jesus says. Instead of condemnation, he experienced redemption; instead of seeking to justify himself in the eyes of God, he receives justification as a gift from Christ. He summed up how this transformation happened for him in these words:

> The human race has nothing to boast about to God, but you, God has made members of Christ Jesus and by God's doing he has become our wisdom, and our virtue, and our holiness, and our freedom (1Corinthians 1:30-31).

The revelation of the body of Christ

What a liberation that was for Paul, when he believed and accepted that God had made him a member of Christ's body and that all the holiness and love of God, which is in Christ, was now also in him! He believed that now he, together with all the other disciples of Jesus, the ones he was hunting down to imprison are, in fact, the body of Christ in this world.

Saul received, on the road to Damascus, the blinding revelation that the Jesus who had been crucified, whose resurrection from the dead his disciples were proclaiming, was truly alive and that his disciples had, in some way beyond his understanding, become his body in this world. He would never forget being blinded by that dazzling light and those words that the voice spoke when he asked him, "Who are you, Lord?" Those words, "I am Jesus and you are persecuting me", were imprinted so deeply in Paul's mind and heart that he became the great evangelist and the teacher of the wonderful divine truth that the Church is the body of Christ in this world. To persecute the Church is to persecute Christ. In all his letters to the newly established Churches in Corinth, or Galatia, in Rome or in Ephesus, Paul kept reminding the faithful that they are "the body of Christ" in this world. He said to the Corinthians, "You together are Christ's body, but each of you is a different part of it" (1 Corinthians 12:27); to the Colossians he wrote, "Now the Church is his body, he is its head" (Colossians 1:18); to the Romans he wrote, "Just as each of our bodies has several parts and each part has a separate function, so all of us, in union with Christ, form one body, and as parts of it we belong to each other (Romans 12:5); to the Galatians he said, "All baptised in Christ, you have all clothed yourselves in Christ, and there are no more distinctions between Jew and Greek, slave and free, male and female, but all of you are one in Christ Jesus" (Galatians 3:27-28). Paul can now only see baptised men and women as the body of Christ in this world. That is why he loved to share with them the great mercy he experienced when Jesus revealed himself to him and when he was baptised by Ananias. Since God embraced him with so much mercy in Christ, despite all the harm he had inflicted on Christ's Church, there is no sin that the God of mercy will refuse to forgive when we come seeking his forgiveness. To emphasise this truth Paul wrote to Timothy, "Jesus Christ meant to make me the greatest evidence of his inexhaustible patience for all the other people who would later have to trust in him to come to eternal life" (I Timothy 1-16).

Letting go of guilt

There is no sin, no matter how grave, that God will not forgive once the contrite heart asks for forgiveness. And when God forgives, the sin is gone, totally removed from the heart. As the psalm says, "as far as the east is from the west, so far does he remove our sins" (Psalm 103:12). It is, therefore, very sad when someone holds on to a feeling of guilt even though the person has confessed the sin and God has forgiven him or her. That feeling of guilt easily turns into a sense that one hasn't really been forgiven. And then one can quickly lose the joy of the Lord. It is worth remembering, whenever we consciously repent of our sins, that Jesus says, "There will be more rejoicing in heaven over one repentant sinner than over the ninety-nine virtuous men who have no need of repentance" (Luke 15:7). Jesus wants us to share in that rejoicing. And St Paul, despite seeing himself as "the greatest sinner", could say that "we are filled with joyful trust in God, through our Lord Jesus Christ, through whom we have already gained our reconciliation" (Romans 5:8-11). And so he urges us to rejoice: "Rejoice in the Lord always; and again I say rejoice" (Philippians 4:4).

Clinging to a sense of guilt, after truly repenting for one's sins, robs the person of joy, of the very capacity to rejoice in the Lord. Worse than that, it can even lead to doubting God's mercy. When one explores with the person why he or she doubts God's mercy, one often discovers a very subtle form of pride that whispers to the person that his or her sin is so grave that even God can't forgive it!

Paul's rejoicing, then, in being "the greatest sinner" is a very important witness for us. Pope Francis has taken that witness to heart. When he was interviewed by a fellow Jesuit in September 2013 he was asked, "Who is Jorge Mario Bergoglio?" And he answered, "I am a sinner." This is the most accurate definition. It is not a figure of speech, a literary genre. "I am a sinner".[1] Francis often says "I am a sinner whom the Lord regards". While speaking to some 4000 prisoners during his visit to Bolivia, Pope Francis began his talk with these words:

> You may be asking yourselves: Who is this man standing before us. I would like to reply to that question with something absolutely certain about my own life. The man standing before you is a man who has experienced forgiveness. A man who was and is saved from his many sins. That is who I am. I don't have much to give you or to offer you, but I want to share with you what I do have and what I love. It is Jesus Christ, the mercy of the Father.[2]

What a profound and simple way to acknowledge that Jesus Christ has come to save sinners and that we are all sinners. By the mercy and love of God we can now be repentant sinners. Then, as we repent our sins there is joy in heaven and joy in our own hearts.

Balance

St Paul was able to keep the balance between believing in his heart that he was the greatest sinner and that God had shown him mercy. He wrote:

> But God loved us with so much love that he was generous with his mercy: when we were dead through our sins, he brought us to life with Christ – it is through grace that you have been saved – and raised us up with him and gave us a place with him in heaven, in Christ Jesus (Ephesians 2: 4-6).

1   *America* Magazine 30 September 2013
2   Zenit. Org, 10 July 2015

Paul, the greatest sinner, is full of joy because he knows that he has been brought to life and now lives in Christ, Indeed he says, "I have been crucified with Christ and I live now not with my own life but with the life of Christ who lives in me. The life I now live in this body I live in faith: faith in the Son of God who loved me and who sacrificed himself for my sake" (Galatians 2:20). His faith assures Paul that he can joyfully boast of being the greatest sinner because it is Christ himself who lives in him. He lives with the very life of Christ. We too have Christ's life in us and Christ wants to live his life to the full in us: his life of love and peace, of mercy and kindness. That is why St Paul can urge us "to rejoice always in the Lord". Because we are in the Lord, like St Paul, we can be aware that we are sinners and rejoice as we give thanks to God for his great mercy and love.

Our faith now makes it possible for us to open our whole being to this life that Christ lives in us. As St John Paul II said:

> Redemption is a truth, a reality, in the name of which we must feel ourselves called, and called with effectiveness.... Christ's words are not a call hurled into emptiness... The words of Christ testify that the original power (and thus also grace) of the mystery of creation becomes for each one of us the power (that is, the grace) of the mystery of redemption.[3]

Notice those words, "Christ's words are not a call hurled into emptiness". Christ's words are the power of God calling us. Each of us is called by God the Father to live the very life of Christ the Son of God in this world now.

Hardening one's heart

The fact that we are sinners is no obstacle to living the life of Christ. The only obstacle is hardening one's heart and refusing to repent and

---

3   St John Paul II, *Theology of the Body*, Pauline Press, Boston 2006, 46: 4,

ask for God's mercy. The deepest longing in the heart of God is that we do not harden our hearts. God teaches us to pray for this grace. Each morning, in the Divine Office of the Church, we hear this plea from God: "O that today you would listen to my voice! Harden not your hearts" (Psalm 94:4). As Cardinal Schoenborn writes:

> Nothing makes hearts harder than self-righteousness. Self-justification is the beginning of all hardness of heart toward others. Nothing opens the floodgates of mercy faster than repentance and the acknowledgement of one's own guilt.[4]

The example of St Paul, always reminding us that he is the greatest sinner, should encourage us to give up all self-justification and accept that we too are sinners and that our justification comes, not from ourselves but from Christ our Lord. Every time we celebrate Mass we acknowledge our sinful state as we say "I confess to almighty God and to you my brothers and sisters that I have greatly sinned, in my thoughts and in my words, in what I have done and in what I have failed to do, through my fault, through my fault, through my most grievous fault." There is no vain attempt at self-justification in that confession! Acknowledging our sinfulness opens our hearts to be filled with the love and mercy of God as we listen to God's word during Mass and receive the body and blood of Christ in Holy Communion.

The light of faith exposes sin

From time to time we meet people who deeply resent being reminded that we are all sinners. They seem to feel judged by this truth of our faith. Rather than being a judgement of God, it is a revelation of God. In his great mercy and love for us, God makes us aware that we are sinners and that Christ came to save us. The Catechism of the Catholic Church gives us this clear teaching on how we become aware of sin:

---

4   Christoph Cardinal Schoenborn, *We Have Found Mercy: The Mystery of God's Merciful Love*, Ignatius Press, San Francisco, 2012, p.58

Only the light of divine Revelation clarifies the reality of sin and particularly of the sin committed at mankind's origins. Without the knowledge Revelation gives of God we cannot recognise sin clearly and are tempted to explain it as merely a developmental flaw, a psychological weakness, a mistake, or a necessary consequence of an inadequate social structure, etc. Only in the knowledge of God's plan for man can we grasp that sin is an abuse of the freedom that God gives to created persons so that they are capable of loving him and loving one another.[5]

God in his mercy reveals to us the true nature and the origin of sin, not to leave us feeling hopeless and helpless, but to empower us with the knowledge of our salvation in Christ. St Paul can rejoice in writing:

God loved us with so much love that he was generous with his mercy: when we were dead through our sins, he brought us to life with Christ – it is through grace that you have been saved – and raised us up with him and gave us a place with him in heaven, in Christ Jesus (Ephesians 2:4-6).

If the cause of so much suffering in our world - injustice and discrimination, lies and manipulations of others, violations of human dignity and of life itself - was "developmental flaws or psychological weakness" not even the best psychologists or psychiatrists can effect the change and liberation needed. But because the root cause of all these attacks on human dignity is in sin, especially in that original sin of our First Parents, we find the liberation we need in Christ's redemption. As the Catechism says,

We must know Christ as the source of grace in order to know Adam as the source of sin. The Spirit-Paraclete, sent by the risen Christ, came to "convict the world concerning sin", by revealing him who is its Redeemer.[6]

---

5   *The Catechism of the Catholic Church*, 387
6   *Ibid* 388

God doesn't reveal the nature and cause of sin without at the same time revealing our redemption from sin in Christ. On our part, we cannot redeem ourselves but we can, in faith, accept the redemption that Christ has come to bring us. That is why the Gospel says "Jesus proclaimed the good news from God" (Mark 1:12), the good news of our redemption from sin. As Zachariah, the father of St John the Baptist said, he has "given his people knowledge of salvation through the forgiveness of their sins" (Luke 1:77).

Living by the word of God

The first word Jesus spoke to us about our salvation was "men and women do not live on bread alone but on every word that comes from the mouth of God" (Matthew 4:4). That is why God pleads with us to listen to his voice and harden not our hearts. Our salvation comes to us, in the first instance, through hearing and accepting and living by the word of God. Benedict XVI wrote:

> We are offered the merciful possibility of redemption and the start of a new life in Christ. For this reason it is important that the faithful be taught to acknowledge that the root of sin lies in the refusal to hear the word of the Lord and accept in Jesus, the Word of God, the forgiveness which opens us to salvation.[7]

If the root of sin is the refusal to hear the word of God, the eagerness to hear God's word is the great sign of grace, of our willingness to live in God's grace, to live by his word. It is with that eagerness that we seek to listen to the word especially when the Scripture is being proclaimed during the celebration of Holy Mass. The prophet Jeremiah speaks of the hunger we should have to be fed on God's word: "When your words came, I devoured them" (Jeremiah 15:16) .

We know from our own experience that it can be quite difficult to pay attention to the readings from the Holy Scriptures during Mass.

---

7   Pope Benedict XVI, Verbum Domini ; Post-Synodal Exhortation on the Word of God, 26

We can be quite deaf to God's word as we listen to the readings. We need the special grace of the "disciple's ear" to hear the word of God. As Scripture says, "Each morning he wakes me to hear, to listen like a disciple. The Lord God has opened my ear" (Isaiah 50:4). That is the big grace we need if we are to "live by every word that comes from the mouth of God" and if we are to deal effectively with the "root of sin" in our hearts. We pray for the grace of being able to listen. We need the light of the word of God. As the Psalm says, "Your word is a lamp to my feet, a light on my path" (Psalm 119:105). Without that light we stumble on in darkness and we will surely fall. But as we listen to the word, as we open our hearts to receive the word, then the blessing that Jesus promises will be ours: "Blessed are those who hear the word of God and keep it" (Luke 11:28).

The Second Vatican Council gave us very clear teaching on the place that the word of God should have in our lives:

> In the sacred books the Father who is in heaven comes lovingly to meet his children and talks with them. And such is the force and the power of the word of God that it can serve the Church as her support and vigour, and the children of the Church as strength for their faith, food for their soul, and a pure and lasting fount of spiritual life.[8]

We have in the word of God all that we need for living our life in God's presence. It is God "the Father of mercies" who comes to greet us and talk to us. Our interior attitude, as we listen to the scripture proclaimed, should always be "speak Lord your servant is listening". I hear the words with my ears, I receive them into my mind, but it is the Holy Spirit who speaks the divine truth expressed by the human words in my heart. If my heart is closed to the word, I may hear it with my ears, but it will not penetrate to the depths of my being. Because Benedict XVI saw so clearly that "the root of sin is the refusal to hear the word of God" he placed great emphasis on

---

8   Constitution on Divine Revelation 21

the need to help each person to see in the word, God's own remedy for our human weaknesses:

> It is decisive from the pastoral standpoint, to present the word of God in its capacity to enter into dialogue with the everyday problems which people face...We need to make every effort to share the word of God as an openness to our problems, a response to our questions, a broadening of our values and the fulfilment of our aspirations.[9]

Pondering the word of God in our heart, not allowing it to "come in one ear and go out of the other", is the only way to enter into deep peace in our relationship with God. It is in our hearts that we believe that "The Lord is compassion and love, slow to anger and rich in mercy" (Psalm 103:8).

St Paul was able to proclaim that "mercy was shown to me". When Jesus spoke to him on the road to Damascus and when Paul, as a result, received baptism at the hands of Ananias, he became a "new man". That was the way he began to understand himself:

> For anyone who is in Christ, there is a new creation; the old creation has gone, and now the new one is here. It is all God's work. It was God who reconciled us to himself through Christ and gave us the work of handing on this reconciliation. In other words, God in Christ was reconciling the world to himself, not holding anyone's faults against them, and he has entrusted to us the news that they are reconciled. So we are ambassadors for Christ; it is as though God were appealing through us, and the appeal that we make in Christ's name is: be reconciled to God. For our sake God made the sinless one into sin, so that in him we might become the goodness of God (2 Corinthians 5:17-21).

---

9   Benedict XVI, Verbum Domini, Post-Synodal Exhortation on the Word of God, 2010, para 23

We can begin to see how Paul, convinced that he was "the greatest sinner" was yet so full of joy and confidence in God. He had experienced God's mercy; he had "become a new creation". He believed that "God in Christ was not holding anyone's faults against them". The mercy that had been shown to him assured him that he could now "become the goodness of God".

That same mercy has been shown to us. We can now combine the awareness of our own sinfulness with joy in being embraced by "the Father of mercies".

Personal spiritual exercise

Centre yourself; sitting upright; breathing rhythmically; clearing your mind of all preoccupations.

Bring yourself to bodily stillness.

Now say in your heart "mercy has been shown to me".

Experience the Father of mercies filling you with his mercy.

Be still for some time in the presence of the God of mercy and compassion and receive his love.

Now focus again on your breathing as you relax in God's presence.

And bring yourself gently back to the world.

This spiritual exercise will deepen your awareness of being in the presence of the God of mercy and make you more grateful for the mercy you have received from God.

— Chapter Four —

Merciful like the Father[1]

Speaking of the peace that mercy brings Jesus says, "Blessed are the merciful, for they shall receive mercy" (Matthew 5:7). And then he tells us what to do with the mercy of God that we received: "Be merciful as your heavenly Father is merciful" (Luke 6:36). Jesus believes that we can have in our hearts for others the very same mercy that God the Father has in his heart for us. That is his very high opinion of each of us. He believes you and I can achieve this high degree of mercy for others. He also expects that we are capable of loving one another in the same way in which he loves us, So, he says to us, "This is my commandment: love one another, as I have loved you" (John 15:12). And, the most amazing expectation of all is that Jesus believes that we are capable of loving our enemies and so he says to us,

> You have learnt how it was said, You must love your neighbour and hate your enemy. But I say this to you: love your enemies and pray for those who persecute you; in this way you will be children of your Father in heaven, for he causes his sun to rise on the bad as well as the good and his rain to fall on honest and dishonest alike (Matthew 5:43-45).

In expressing these very high expectations of what we are capable of doing, Jesus is reminding us of our true identity. God is our heavenly Father and we are his sons and daughters. We have the very life of the heavenly Father within us. We have been born again

---

1   Pope Francis says that *Merciful like the Father* is the motto he has chosen for the Holy Year of Mercy. Cf. Misercordiae Vultus, para 14

"through water and the Spirit" (John 3:5). Because we are the sons and daughters of the Father we can be like the Father in the way we love. As St Paul says, "The love of God has been poured into our hearts by the Holy Spirit who has been given us" (Romans 5:5). It is with this love poured into our hearts, God's own love, that we can now love even our enemies. And it is with the very mercy that God the Father has shown to us that we can now show mercy to others. That is why Pope Francis chose Merciful like the Father as the motto for the Holy Year of Mercy.

Mercy: synthesis of the Gospel

Speaking to the Priests of the Sacred Heart Congregation in Rome, Pope Francis gave them this very clear teaching on mercy:

> Mercy is the word that synthesises the Gospel. We can say that it is the "face" of Christ, the face that he showed when he went out to everyone, when he healed the sick, when he sat at table with sinners, and especially when, nailed to the cross, he forgave: there we have the face of divine mercy. And the Lord calls you to be "channels" of this love in the first place, to the last, to the very poor, who - in his eyes - are the privileged. Let yourselves continually question situations of fragility and poverty with which you meet, and try to offer in suitable ways the witness of charity that the Spirit pours into your hearts (cf. Romans 5:5).[2]

When we try to be merciful to others we are showing them the face of Christ. We become witnesses to Christ. Even if we don't always succeed in making a generous, merciful response in some situations; the very fact that we are trying, that we are aware that mercy has been shown to us and that we must respond with mercy, is in itself a sign that we are on the right road. The Holy Spirit will "help us in our weakness" and we will grow in mercy as we persevere in doing

---

2   Pope Francis, Address to the General Chapter of the Priests of the Sacred Heart, zenith.org, 5 June 2015

our best. Christ says to us: "Blessed are the merciful: they shall have mercy shown to them" (Matthew 5:7).

God's gift

The love of God that has been poured into our hearts has been given to us as a gift. We share this gift of God with others when we love, and especially when our love takes the form of forgiveness. When we forgive we are being merciful as our heavenly Father is merciful. This is so central to our Christian life that Jesus put the forgiveness of others at the very heart of our relationship with God. In his great prayer, the Lord's Prayer, he teaches us to say, "Forgive us our trespasses as we forgive those who trespass against us." Jesus not only asks us to be as merciful as the heavenly Father, he also shows us the very specific way in which we can show that mercy, namely by forgiving one another. He emphasized this teaching very strongly when he said: "Yes, if you forgive others their failings, your heavenly Father will forgive you yours; but if you do not forgive others, your Father will not forgive your failings either" (Matthew 6:14).

St Peter had a problem with someone in his life. He asked the Lord, "How often must I forgive my brother if he wrongs me? As often as seven times?" Jesus answered, "Not seven, I tell you, but seventy-seven times" (Matthew 18:21-22). We can imagine Peter's shock at Jesus' answer. He thought he was being very generous with his forgiveness by saying that perhaps he should forgive seven times. But Jesus is saying that there is no limit to forgiveness. Jesus is also implying that forgiveness from the heart should be unconditional while Peter, in his generosity, was putting a big condition in place. No more than seven times! To help Peter understand what true forgiveness is like Jesus told him a story, a parable. It is a long parable, but as we are pondering God's mercy for us and how we show mercy to one another, it is worth telling in full. Jesus says:

The kingdom of heaven may be compared to a king who decided to settle his accounts with his servants. When the reckoning began, they brought him a man who owed ten thousand talents; but he had no means of paying, so his master gave orders that he should be sold, together with his wife and children and all his possessions, to meet the debt. At this, the servant threw himself down at his master's feet. "Give me time" he said "and I will pay the whole sum". And the servant's master felt so sorry for him that he let him go and cancelled the debt. Now as this servant went out, he happened to meet a fellow servant who owed him one hundred denarii; and he seized him by the throat and began to throttle him. "Pay what you owe me" he said. His fellow servant fell at his feet and implored him saying, "Give me time and I will pay you". But the other would not agree; on the contrary, he had him thrown into prison till he should pay the debt. His fellow servants were deeply distressed when they saw what had happened, and they went to their master and reported the whole affair to him. Then the master sent for him. "You wicked servant", he said "I cancelled all that debt of yours when you appealed to me. Were you not bound, then, to have pity on your fellow servant just as I had pity on you?" And in his anger the master handed him over to the torturers till he should pay all his debt. And that is how my heavenly Father will deal with you unless you each forgive your brother from your heart (Matthew 18:23-35).

The logic of this parable is compelling. Yet it helps if we look at the three different scenes:

Scene one
The servant who owes an unpayable debt pleads for more time and the king forgives the whole debt. The servant can now walk away a

free man. Having experienced such mercy from his master he would be full of compassion for others who were in debt to him.

Scene two
The forgiven servant now meets a fellow servant and demands repayment of a very small debt and ignores all his pleas for more time. He shows no mercy and insists on his rights.

Scene three
When the master hears how the servant whom he had forgiven such a large debt refused to forgive his fellow servant a trivial debt, he responds in kind to the unforgiving servant.

There is a consistency in God's forgiving relationship with us. As we forgive, he forgives; as we refuse to forgive, he withdraws his forgiveness. We cannot hold on to the divine forgiveness if we refuse to share it. The Catechism of the Catholic Church clarifies the implications of the parable for us in this way:

> The outpouring of mercy cannot penetrate our hearts as long as we have not forgiven those who have trespassed against us. Love, like the body of Christ, is indivisible; we cannot love the God we cannot see if we do not love the brother or sister we do see. In refusing to forgive our brothers or sisters, our hearts are closed and their hardness makes them impervious to the Father's merciful love; but in confessing our sins our hearts are open to his grace.[3]

The work of grace
Refusing to show God's mercy to those who offend us, after receiving this mercy from God, is spiritually very dangerous. By closing our hearts to our brother or sister we cannot hold on to the mercy that we ourselves have received from God. That is why Jesus says to us very insistently "cut off from me you can do nothing" (John 15:5). Being merciful as our heavenly Father is merciful is a work

---

3   Catechism of the Catholic Church, para 2840

of divine grace in us. If we live in grace we can do it; if we reject grace we cannot do it.

God has made it possible for us to live in grace because he has made us members of Christ's body. To use Jesus' own image:

> I am the true vine...Make your home in me, as I make mine in you. As a branch cannot bear fruit all by itself, but must remain part of the vine, neither can you unless you remain in me... Whoever remains in me, with me in him, bears fruit in plenty; for cut off from me you can do nothing (John 15:1. 4-5).

When it comes to trying to be "as merciful as our heavenly Father" we experience the truth of what Christ is saying to us. We cannot be like the Father if we are cut off from Christ because it is only in and through Christ that we are the sons and daughters of the Father. As St Paul reminds us: "Now you together are Christ's body; but each of you is a different part of it" (1 Corinthians 12:27). Our relationship with Christ is so intimate and close that it can only be compared to the relationship that a member of the body has with the head, or the relationship that the branch of the vine has with the vine. We share in the very nature of Christ, in the very nature of God. That is what we pray for in every Mass as we say "through the mystery of this water and wine may we come to share in the divinity of Christ who humbled himself to share in our humanity".

Because Christ shares with us his very divinity he can ask us to be as merciful as the heavenly Father is merciful and he can ask us to love one another as he loves us. He is not asking the impossible of us. Rather, he is asking us to be true to ourselves: we have been "born again... through water and the Spirit" (John 3:5); we are "the temple of the Holy Spirit" (1 Corinthians 6:19); we have "the mind of Christ" (1 Corinthians 2:16). Because we have "the mind of Christ" we can see the meaning and the purpose of our lives in this world as Christ sees them. We don't have to look out on our relationship with others through a lens distorted by our own sinfulness. Christ has given us his own mind so that we can begin to see our life as he sees it, and see what it means to be merciful, as he sees it. We can have no greater success in this world than to live a life that Christ acknowledges as merciful. Indeed, in St Matthew's Gospel, Jesus tells us that mercy will be the standard through which he will judge the world on the Last Day:

> Then the King will say to those on his right hand, "Come, you whom my Father has blessed, take for your heritage the kingdom prepared for you since the foundation of the world. For I was hungry and you gave me food; I was thirsty and you gave me drink; I was a stranger and you made me welcome; naked and you clothed me, sick and you visited me, in prison and you came to see me… In so far as you did this to one of the least of these my brothers of mine, you did it to me". And to those who have not lived a life of merciful love Christ will say, "Go away from me, with your curse upon you, to the eternal fire prepared for the devil and his angels. For I was hungry and you never gave me food; I was thirsty and you never gave me anything to drink; I was a stranger and you never made me welcome; naked and you never clothed me, sick and in prison and you never visited me… In so far as you neglected to do this to one of the least of these, you neglected to do it to me" (Matthew 25:34-46).

The mind of Christ

St Paul tells us that "we are those who have the mind of Christ" (1 Corinthians 2:16). Without the "mind of Christ" we cannot see Christ in the stranger and the beggar, in the outcast and the sinner, in the people who upset or offend us. That is why Jesus stresses, "cut off from me you can do nothing". Without Christ, without experiencing the mercy of God given to us through Christ, we cannot live the life of Christ in this world, Christ makes it possible for us to live the life of grace by making us his body in his world. As St Paul says, "Now you together are Christ's body; but each of you is a different part of it" (1 Corinthians 12:27). This is why Christ can have such high expectations of us. He lives in us and we live in him, and he will do in us the merciful and loving deeds that show that we are sons and daughters of the heavenly Father. As St John Eudes wrote:

> Remember that our Lord Jesus Christ is your true head and that you are his members. He is to you as the head is to the members of the body; all that is his is yours. His spirit, his heart, his body, his soul, all his faculties, all are to be used by you as if they were your own, so that serving him you may praise him, love him, glorify him. For your part, you are to him as a member to the head, and he earnestly desires to use all your faculties as if they were his own for the service and glorification of his Father.[4]

Jesus responds with mercy

Love of neighbour and mercy for the afflicted are by their very nature concrete virtues. We don't love humanity, nor have compassion on humanity. We love the individual person we encounter, the neighbour, and we have compassion on the individual suffering person that we can help. The fact that I cannot help every suffering person at this moment is no justification for me not trying to assist the person who turns to me for help. When a lawyer tried to catch Jesus out on this kind of an issue, Jesus didn't engage him in a theoretical discussion about the law. He told him a story, a parable. St Luke records the scene:

> There was a lawyer who, to disconcert him, stood up and said to him, "Master, what must I do to inherit eternal life?" He said to him. "What is written in the Law? What do you read there?" He replied, "You must love the Lord

---

4   Office of Readings, 20 August, Feast of St John Eudes

your God with all your heart, with all your soul, with all your strength, and with all your mind, and your neighbour as yourself". "You have answered right" said Jesus, "do this and life is yours". But the man was anxious to justify himself and said to Jesus, "And who is my neighbour?" (Luke10:25-29).

The commandment to love one's neighbour as oneself didn't sit easily with that lawyer. He was looking for some loopholes in this law. Is every living person your neighbour? How could you love everyone as you love yourself? In response Jesus told his famous parable of the Good Samaritan:

> A man was once on his way down from Jerusalem to Jericho and fell into the hands of brigands; they took all he had, beat him and then made off, leaving him half dead. Now a priest happened to be travelling down the same road, but when he saw the man, he passed by on the other side. In the same way a Levite who came to the place saw him, and passed by on the other side. But a Samaritan traveller who came upon him was moved with compassion when he saw him. He went up and bandaged his wounds, pouring oil and wine on them. He then lifted him onto his own mount, carried him to the inn and looked after him... "Which of these three, do you think, proved himself a neighbour to the man who fell into the brigand's hands?" "The one who took pity on him" he replied. Jesus said to him, "Go, and do the same yourself" (Luke 10:29 –37).

Notice how adroitly Jesus has rephrased the lawyer's question, "Who is my neighbour?" by asking him "Which of the three proved himself a neighbour to the man who fell into the brigand's hands?" Jesus is saying to him that it is not humanity in general that we are told to love as ourselves. I become a neighbour to the person I meet. He or she is the neighbour I love as myself. The Samaritan, we are told, was "moved with compassion" when he saw the half-dead man on the road. He didn't harden his heart as the other two had done. He loved his neighbour by being merciful to him. When I meet a poor person begging on the street, the fact that there are many beggars in the world is no justification for me not to be a generous neighbour to this one poor beggar who looks to me for help.

Compassion and mercy: the mother love of God

Compassion and mercy are used interchangeably in the New Testament to describe the loving and tender responses that Jesus made to the people who cried to him for help. The Gospels tell us frequently that Jesus "was moved with compassion". The Greek word translated "compassion" in the Gospels literally means "to be moved in one's bowels". In the ancient Hebrew world "the bowels" were seen as the centre of the emotions of kindness, benevolence and pity. Today, we see "the heart" as the centre of these emotions. We can say that compassion is a deep "gut feeling", an inner feeling that motivates action. Jesus, when moved with compassion, acted: cf. Matthew 9:36; 14:14; Mark 1:41; 6:34; 8:2; Luke 7:13. He reached out, touched and healed those who appealed to him and, when necessary, he fed 5000 with five loaves and two fish. He had compassion for the widow whose only son had died and he raised him from the dead (Luke 7:11-17). He opened his heart to those in need. Indeed, the Hebrew word from which our word "compassion" is derived means "womb". Cardinal Kasper writes:

> It is characteristic of the Old and the New Testament that they use the expression *rachamim* for "compassion" and, for that matter, also for "mercy". This word is derived from *rechem*, which means "womb".[5]

Compassion is, then, "mother love". Christ's compassion reveals "the mother love of God" for his people. As the Catechism of the Catholic Church teaches:

5   Cardinal Walter Kasper, *Mercy: The Essence of the Gospel and the Key to Christian Life*, Paulist Press, New York, 2014, p.42

God's parental tenderness can also be expressed by the image of motherhood, which emphasizes God's immanence, the intimacy between Creator and creature.[6]

The prophet Isaiah makes a direct connection between a mother's love and God's love: "Does a woman forget her baby at the breast, or fail to cherish the son of her womb? Yet even if these forget, I will never forget you" (Isaiah 49:15). The image of mother may speak to you more clearly about the love, the compassion, and tenderness of God. God uses this image to encourage us: "At her breast will her nurslings be carried and fondled in her lap. Like a son comforted by his mother will I comfort you" (Isaiah 66:13). And we read in the psalm, "Enough for me to keep my soul tranquil and quiet like a child in its mother's arms, as content as a child that has been weaned" (Psalm 131:2).

When Jesus was moved with compassion he opened his heart to the person in need. He revealed the mother love of God. The opposite of opening one's heart is closing one's heart. St John uses this image when he writes, "If a man who was rich enough in this world's goods saw that one of his brothers was in need, but closed his heart to him, how could the love of God be living in him?" (1 John 3:17). We cannot be merciful as our heavenly Father is merciful if we close our hearts to the person in need.

The word mercy, synonymous with compassion, has its roots in the Latin word *misercordia*. It is composed from two Latin words: *miseri*, which means the unfortunate, and *cor*, which means heart. So, literally our word "mercy" means "having a heart for the unfortunate". St Thomas Aquinas wrote:

> That person is called merciful because he has a heart (cor) with misery, and is affected by another's sadness or another's plight as though it were his own. He identifies himself with the other and springs to the rescue; this is the effect of mercy.[7]

---

6   Catechism of the Catholic Church, 239
7   St Thomas Aquinas, Summa Theologica, 1 – 2, q. 21 a. 3

Christ, "the face of the Father's mercy", was "the man for others". He sprang to their help. In asking us to be "as merciful as his heavenly Father" he is inviting us to spring to the help of those in need. Indeed, Pope Francis is encouraging the whole Church to be the "Church of mercy". He writes:

> The Church must be a place of mercy freely given, where everyone can feel welcomed, loved and encouraged to live the good life of the Gospel.[8]

Church is a mystery

The Church is not an international, corporate organisation, although it exists in every country of the world. Nor is the Church, as Pope Francis is fond of saying, a big NGO, a non-governmental organisation helping people in need all over the world, even though it provides more help through its members who teach and nurse and work for human development on every level, than all the NGOs put together. The Vatican Council taught us that the "Church is a people made one with the unity of the Father, the Son and the Holy Spirit".[9] As God's people who have been redeemed by Christ, who have had their sins forgiven by Christ and who seek to show the love of Christ to others, the Church is the sacrament of Christ in the world. She is "the sacrament of mercy" in the world today. In encountering the Church, the people of God, individuals and whole communities should be encountering the mercy of God. As Pope Francis says:

> Wherever the Church is present, the mercy of the Father must be evident. In our parishes, communities, associations and movements, in a word wherever there are Christians, everyone should find an oasis of mercy.[10]

Mercy should be the "public face" of the Church of Christ because Christ is the "face of the mercy of the Father". If people do not feel embraced by mercy as they approach the Church they will never

---

8   Pope Francis, *The Joy of the Gospel*, 114)
9   Second Vatican Council, Constitution on the Church, 4
10 Pope Francis, Misericordiae Vultus: Bull of Indiction of the Extraordinary Jubilee Year of Mercy, 12

enter into communion with the Church. People meet the Church in its individual members, in the parishes, priests and people. As members of the Church, our witness should speak clearly about the mercy of God for each individual to those who are seeking Christ and a deeper meaning in life, no matter what his or her circumstances may be. The bigger the sinner, the bigger the welcome! We are not a Church that condemns others; we are a Church that encourages everyone, a Church that believes that God, who has been patient and forgiving in the way he deals with us, will be equally patient and forgiving with every single person, even with those who at the present may seem to be enemies of the Church, as St Paul once was. Pope Francis profiles the type of Christians who are needed today:

> We need Christians who make God's mercy and tenderness for every creature visible to the men of our day. We all know that the crisis of modern man is not superficial but profound. That is why the New Evangelisation, while it calls us to have the courage to swim against the tide and to be converted from idols to the true God, cannot but use a language of mercy, which is expressed in gestures and attitudes even before words.[11]

If we are going to be "merciful as our heavenly Father is merciful" we cannot "close our hearts" to those in need. The mercy that we ourselves have received from God must be shared with those who need to receive our mercy. St John Paul II was very specific on this point:

> Jesus Christ taught that man not only receives and experiences the mercy of God, but that he is also called "to practise mercy" towards others. The Church sees in these words a call to action, and she tries to practise mercy.[12]

---

11 Address to the Pontifical Council for promoting the New Evangelisation, October 14, 2013.
12 St John Paul II, *On the Mercy of God*, 14

The corporal and spiritual works of mercy

In our Catholic tradition we have always talked about the "works of mercy" which have been divided into two categories, corporal works of mercy which meet the material needs of others, and spiritual works of mercy that seek to respond to the spiritual needs of others. Speaking of these works of mercy Pope Francis says:

> It is my burning desire that, during this Jubilee, the Christian people may reflect on the corporal and spiritual works of mercy. It will be a way to reawaken our conscience, too often grown dull in the face of poverty. And let us enter more deeply into the heart of the Gospel where the poor have a special experience of God's mercy. Jesus introduces us to these works of mercy in his preaching so that we can know whether or not we are living as his disciples.[13]

These corporal and spiritual works of mercy, therefore, could be the guiding principles for parishes and communities as they plan to show mercy to all who come to them for corporal or spiritual help. In each category there are seven specific works of mercy. Let us refresh our memories:

The seven corporal works of mercy:

To feed the hungry
To give drink to the thirsty
To clothe the naked
To shelter the homeless
To visit the sick
To visit the imprisoned
To bury the dead.

The seven spiritual works of mercy:

To instruct the ignorant
To counsel the doubtful

---

13 Misericordiae Vultus 15

To admonish sinners
To bear wrongs patiently
To forgive offences willingly
To comfort the afflicted
To pray for the living and the dead

Outreach to the poor and abandoned

Throughout the ages, and especially in our own times, Christian men and women have faithfully devoted their energies, their wealth and their talents, to engaging in these works of mercy all over the world. Blessed Mother Teresa became, in our own day, the iconic figure of these works of mercy. Many of our parishes have St Vincent de Paul Societies. We see their members after Mass, outside churches all over the country, with their collection boxes. The pound or the fifty pence coins that the Mass goers put in those boxes feed a multitude of hungry people. It is so beautiful to see parents give their children coins for the collection box. This is a true formation of the children in the works of mercy. Dr Michael Thio, President of the International Confederation of the Society of St Vincent de Paul, speaking about their work at the Vatican in February 2013, gave the following report:

> Since our humble beginnings 180 years ago we are today present in 148 countries, with 780,000 members spread over 70,000 conferences, 1.3 million volunteers and serving over 30 million poor. The Society is involved in a wide range and variety of tasks and activities from the provision of food, clothing and necessities to the needy, homes for the poor and homeless, response to natural disasters in emergency reliefs and rehabilitation projects, assistance to refugees that emerged from political conflicts, engaged in systemic change programs in education, self-help projects, micro-financing, counselling and many others. Among many other assistance projects for last year, special mention is made

to emergency relief provided to over 20 countries affected by natural disasters along with rehabilitation projects, assistance in the famine in the Horn of Africa, food and crops programs, provision for rebuilding, renovation and construction of houses and notably support for a project in the construction of an indoor playground of a kindergarten due to the Tsunami tragedy in Fukushima, Japan, that is subjected to nuclear radiation.[14]

What an extraordinary manifestation of how to be "as merciful as the heavenly Father".

Mary's Meals

A young Scottish layman, Magnus MacFarlane-Barrow, from his home in the Scottish Highlands in 2002, began a charitable project which he called Mary's Meals. The purpose of this charity was to provide 200 hungry children in Malawi with one cooked meal a day at school. He began his work in faith. Today, thirteen years later, Mary's Meals now feeds over 1,000,000 school children in a number of the poorest countries in the world. This has become possible through the generosity of thousands of men and women who generously give a few pounds to support this wonderful charity.[15] Again, we see in Mary's Meals the concrete manifestation of what it means to be "merciful as our heavenly Father is merciful".

Food banks and drop-in centres for the poor and homeless

The needs of the poor have escalated in recent years even in a rich country like Britain where many people have to depend on the charity of others for their very survival. The Trussell Trust[16], for instance, runs a national food bank charity which has provided a three-day supply of basic food to over a million people in a twelve-month

---

14 Zenit.org, 1 February 2013
15 For further information google Mary's Meals
16 www.trusselltrust.org/foodbank-projects

period from 2014 to 2015. Many local charities, in all the churches, have been responding in some way to this great social problem. Charities do not get involved in the political analysis of why, although they would all agree that the ultimate solution has to be political. But the corporal works of mercy, such as feeding the hungry, cannot wait for politicians to come up with solutions. Each one of us is responsible for making whatever contribution we can to alleviate the distress of the hungry and the homeless.

Twenty years ago, the Redemptorists in Clapham Common, London, turned their old school, which had become redundant because of the amalgamation of the two schools of the parish, into a drop-in Day Centre for the poor and homeless. They called the new Centre the Ace of Clubs.[17] The Centre has become a life-saver for many destitute people, providing food, friendship, clothing, laundry, showers, accommodation advice, welfare advice, health care, an optician, education and training, and many other services that are impossible for the poor on their own to access. During the year tens of thousands of meals are served to poor men and women who depend on the Ace of Clubs for their very survival. Men and women are helped back on their feet and receive expert support in finding accommodation and jobs. Similar charities all over London are also engaged in the basic corporal works of mercy, namely feeding the hungry, helping them to find accommodation and employment, health care and literacy skills. They all depend on the generosity of both the big donors, the Charitable Foundation, and the individual parishioners who are willing to give a few pounds for the relief of the hungry.

There are many hundreds of other charities, organisations and societies, all over the Church, feeding the hungry and supporting the sick and the dying. As a Church we have been very faithful to the corporal works of mercy. We have every good reason to thank God for this great grace of fidelity and generosity. It is the living out of the Lord's command: "Be merciful as your heavenly Father is merciful".

---

17 Aceofclubs.org.uk

Whenever you have the opportunity to support one of those charitable organisations that is acting on the Church's behalf it is a great grace to give as generously as you can.

The new evangelisation

One of the great spiritual works of mercy is bringing the good news of Christ's redemption to others. Today the Church is urgently calling on all her members to become active in "the new evangelisation". Pope Francis gave us this rallying call in his great Apostolic Exhortation:

> All the baptised, whatever their position in the Church or their level of instruction in the faith, are agents of evangelisation, and it would be insufficient to envisage a plan of evangelisation carried out by professionals while the rest of the faithful would remain simply passive. The new evangelisation calls for personal involvement on the part of each of the baptised... We no longer say that we are "disciples" and "missionaries" but rather that we are always "missionary disciples".[18]

Being merciful as our heavenly Father is merciful is the compelling reason for sharing our faith with others, for being the "missionary disciples" that Pope Francis calls each of us to be. We seek to make both a personal and a community response. On the personal level we share our faith with the person who expresses any kind of interest. St Peter has this word of encouragement for each of us:

> Simply reverence the Lord Christ in your hearts, and always have your answer ready for people who ask you the reason for the hope that you all have. But give it with courtesy and respect... (1 Peter 3:15).

It is that "courtesy and respect" that invite people to ask about our faith. Indeed, as Pope Francis says, "It is not by proselytising that

---

18 Pope Francis, Evangelii Gaudium: *The Joy of the Gospel*, 119

the Church grows, but by attraction."[19] Most people who join the Church say that it was the example of an individual that first attracted them to consider becoming a Catholic.

As a parish community we have to be "as merciful as our heavenly Father is merciful". All our parishes have to become missionary communities. St John Paul II has this strong word for each parish:

> No Christian community is faithful to its duty unless it is missionary: either it is a missionary community or it is not even a Christian community.[20]

That is the great challenge to our parish communities today. Are we ready to face this challenge? Are we willing to be "as merciful as our heavenly Father" and bring the good news of his salvation to others? What would an evangelising parish look like? Pope Francis gives us a clear picture:

> An evangelising community knows that the Lord has taken the initiative, he has loved us first (cf. 1 John 4:19), and therefore we can move forward, boldly take the initiative, go out to others, seek those who have fallen away, stand at the crossroads and welcome the outcast.[21]

The evangelising initiative is Christ's. But Christ now acts in and through us. We are encouraged "boldly to take the initiative" as we go out in the Lord's name to make disciples. We have to share with others, in the words of the Second Vatican Council, "reasons for living and reasons for hoping"[22]. The human heart longs to know these reasons.

St John Paul II reminds us that "the effectiveness of the Church's organisations, movements, parishes and apostolic works must be measured in the light of this missionary imperative".[23] All the organisations in your parish should have as their ultimate aim the

---

19 Pope Francis, *The Joy of the Gospel*, 14
20 St John Paul II, Message for World Mission Day, 20 October 1991
21 Pope Francis, *The Joy of the Gospel*, 24
22 Church in the Modern World, 31
23 St John Paul II, Mission of the Redeemer, 49

spreading of the Gospel. That is how the community becomes "as merciful as our heavenly Father".

Personal spiritual exercise

Centre yourself; sitting upright; breathing rhythmically; clearing your mind of all preoccupations.

Bring yourself to bodily stillness.

Now hear in your heart the invitation of the Lord: "Be merciful as your heavenly Father is merciful."

Ask the Father of mercies to show you how to be merciful.

Be still for some time in the presence of the God of mercy and compassion and receive his love.

Now focus again on your breathing as you relax in God's presence.

And bring yourself gently back to the world.

This spiritual exercise will deepen your awareness of being in the presence of the God of mercy and will show you how to grow in mercy for someone in your life.

— Chapter Five —

Approaching the throne of grace and mercy

In the Letter to the Hebrews the Holy Spirit gives us this word of encouragement: "Let us be confident, then, in approaching the throne of grace, that we shall have mercy from him and find grace when we are in need of help" (Hebrews 4:16). We have to take that first step of approaching, we have to make the move from being closed in on ourselves, holding on to our guilt and fears, and come confidently to the throne where Christ, the mercy of the Father, embraces us and makes us feel at home. As St Peter assures us, "Once you were outside the mercy and now you have been given mercy" (1 Peter 2:10).

St Leo the Great, speaking about Christ's presence with us today after his Ascension into heaven, said, "The visible presence of the Redeemer passed over into the sacraments."[1] Christ's first disciples had his visible presence with them for three years. They walked the roads of Galilee with him. They saw his great miracles and were encouraged by the gospel, the good news that he was preaching and the wonderful revelation of the God of mercy that he was giving them. But he told them that he would have to leave them. In fact, much to their amazement he said, "It is for your own good that I am going because unless I go, the Advocate will not come to you; but if I do go I will send him to you" (John 16:7). At first the disciples could not absorb what Jesus was saying. What could be better for them than to have the visible presence of Jesus with them always? They were so encouraged by his friendship, so excited by

---

1   Office of Readings, Friday after the Ascension

his wonderful works, so secure in his presence. And yet Jesus, their Lord and master is saying to them, it is better for them not to have his visible presence and to have the invisible presence of the Holy Spirit. They really only began to understand what Jesus was saying when he departed from their midst and sent the Holy Spirit. Then their eyes were opened and they began to see that although Jesus was visibly no longer with them, he was invisibly present in their midst and performing the same great works of mercy through the sacraments that he instituted before he left them. Truly his visible presence had passed over into the sacraments.

In this chapter, we will reflect on how we encounter that wonderful presence of Jesus in the sacrament of reconciliation. For centuries we only spoke about the sacrament of confession and about "going to confession". But today we have various titles for this sacrament. We refer to it as the sacrament of reconciliation, the sacrament of penance, or the sacrament of confession. I will be using these titles of the sacrament interchangeably in these reflections.

An ecumenical experience

Before we consider the sacrament in detail, I wish to share an experience I had while speaking about the healing power of the sacrament of confession to a large group of 150 Presbyterian ministers. I was giving a three-day conference on the Ministry of Healing to this very impressive group of men and women, totally dedicated to bringing Christ's healing love to their people and eager to examine Catholic ways of praying for healing. They made me feel very much at home with them. When I give courses on the Ministry of Healing, I always speak about the healing power of the sacrament of confession and I introduce the talk with a few quotations from Carl Jung, one of the founding fathers of modern psychology. I was somewhat apprehensive about using these quotations from Jung with a group of Presbyterian ministers because, for some who are not Catholics, the Catholic practice of going to confession is a baffling and unnecessary pastoral ritual. Jung himself was a Presbyterian, yet over his many years of psychoanalytical work with patients, he developed a high regard for the Catholic practice of "going to confession". This is the first quotation I use:

> The fact is there are relatively few neurotic Catholics, and yet they are living under the same conditions as we do. They are presumably suffering from the same social conditions and so on, and so one would expect a similar amount of neurosis. There must be something in the cult, in the actual religious practice, which explains that peculiar fact that there are fewer complexes, or that these complexes manifest themselves much less in Catholics than in other people. That something, besides confession, is really the cult itself. It is the Mass.[2]

Jung attributed the fact that "there were relatively few neurotic Catholics" to the liberating power of confession and the Mass which freed them from their guilt and shame. We will look at the Mass in more detail in the next chapter. For Jung, however, confession was the central sacrament in the Catholic tradition that explained why so many Catholics were free from "neurotic manifestations". So he wrote:

> You find the least or smallest number of complex manifestations in practising Catholics, far more in Protestants, and most in Jews... So there must be something in the Catholic Church which accounts for this peculiar fact. Of course, we think in the first place of confession.[3]

The conference listened to these quotations from Jung with great interest. We had a very lively discussion after my presentation. There was real interest in how the Catholic Church today understands this sacrament of confession. One lady minister came forward to the

---

2   C. G. Jung, *The Collected Works*, Routledge & Kegan Paul Ltd, London 1977, Vol. 18, para 613
3   *Ibid* Vol. 18. 612/3

microphone and told the whole group about an experience she had the previous week. One of her parishioners came to see her. She said, "He had big trouble and I knew right well that he really wanted to make a confession, but he didn't know what to do. So, I said to him, 'Jack, just treat me as if I were a Catholic priest and I will hear your confession'". Despite the fact that the Presbyterian Church doesn't have a rite of confession to the minister, the whole conference was very relaxed about what she had said. Indeed, some of them said to me that the loss of the practice of confession at the time of the Reformation was a great pastoral impoverishment in their ministry.

The confessor

Some people, I know, have had rather bad experiences of "making their confession". We come to celebrate the sacrament of confession not to be told off by the priest, but to be received and embraced by "the Father of mercies", just as the prodigal son in the parable of God's mercy was embraced by his father. The rite of the sacrament of reconciliation describes the confessor's role in this way:

> By receiving repentant sinners and leading them to the light of the truth, the confessor fulfils a paternal function: he reveals the heart of the Father and shows the image of Christ the Good Shepherd.[4]

It is the heart of God the Father that the penitent encounters in the sacrament of reconciliation. Jesus illustrates the welcome home we receive from the Father in his parable of the prodigal son. Remember how in the parable (see chapter 3) the father spots the returning son while he is still far off and he runs to embrace him. He was able to spot him at a distance because every day he was watching for his return. We often speak about "going to confession" but in reality it is the Father who, watching for us and our approach to "the throne of mercy", runs to meet us. The Father is watching for us to make

---

4   New Rite of Reconciliation, no. 10

the first move. He patiently waits for us freely to decide that we want to approach "the throne of grace and mercy". Then he rushes to embrace us and fill us with the Holy Spirit.

The work of the Holy Spirit

The sacrament of reconciliation gives us a fresh infilling of the Holy Spirit. When Jesus appeared to his disciples after the resurrection on Easter Sunday evening, he greeted them with the words: "Peace be with you" and then, we are told, he breathed on them and said,

> Receive the Holy Spirit.
> For those whose sins you forgive,
> they are forgiven;
> for those whose sins you retain,
> they are retained (John 20:21-23).

As the priest absolves the penitent he recalls this infilling with the Spirit. He says:

> God the Father of mercies, through the death and resurrection of his Son Jesus, has reconciled the world to himself and sent the Holy Spirit among us for the forgiveness of sins.

The Father of mercies fills the heart of the penitent with the Holy Spirit and takes away all sins. The repentant sinner is completely cleansed in the sanctifying waters of the Spirit as the priest says, in the name of Jesus, "I absolve you from all your sins in the name of the Father and of the Son and of the Holy Spirit." In that very moment it is the "Father of mercies" who welcomes and embraces the repentant penitent. All sins are forgiven and the wounds of sin are healed.

In the very act of absolving the penitent the priest emphasises the fact that it is the Holy Spirit, now present with us in Christ's sacrament of reconciliation, who is the forgiver of sins.

The Holy Spirit is the New Covenant

At the Last Supper, Christ proclaimed the new covenant between God and us when he said, "This cup is the new covenant in my blood which will be poured out for you" (Luke 22:20). The sacrifice of his life on the cross, which he offered to the Father for our sake, reconciled us with God and gained for us a new covenant, a new and personal relationship with God our Father. St Thomas Aquinas, one of our great theologians, writing in the thirteenth century said, "The new covenant consists in the inpouring of the Holy Spirit";[5] and in another commentary St Thomas wrote, "As the Holy Spirit works in us charity which is the fullness of the Law, he himself is the New Covenant".[6]

When Christ fulfilled his promise and sent the Holy Spirit to the disciples they began to understand why it was better for them personally that he went away. The invisible presence of the Holy Spirit in their minds and hearts and in their community meant that Christ was with them now in a new way and they were with him in a new way. They realised that now their new union with Christ was so close and so intimate that they had become the body of Christ in this world. As St Paul preached so constantly: "Now you together are Christ's body; but each of you is a different part of it" (1 Corinthians 12:27).

A sacrament is a visible sign of invisible grace. We see the visible sign with our physical eyes. But it is with the "eyes of faith" that we see the invisible grace of the Holy Spirit present in the sacrament of the New Covenant and being communicated to us. For instance, the pouring of water over the head of the person being baptised with the words "I baptise you in the name of the Father and of the Son and of the Holy Spirit" is the visible sign that we see at a baptism. The invisible grace of the person being filled with the Holy Spirit, "being born again through water and the Spirit" (John 3:5), can only be seen "with the eyes of faith". We believe that God's redeeming love

---

5   St Thomas Aquinas, Heb. Cap. 8. Lect. 2
6   St Thomas Aquinas, 2 Cor. Cap. 3, lect. 2

comes to us in that visible sign. The visible sign in the celebration of the sacrament of reconciliation is the penitent kneeling or sitting with the priest, asking for a blessing and then simply confessing whatever sins are troubling his or her conscience at that moment and the priest pronouncing those words of absolution.

Acknowledging before God that we are sinners is not engaging in negative thinking about oneself. It is the very opposite. It is God who reveals to us that we are sinners and that the deepest desire in the heart of God is that we welcome the grace of reconciliation that God offers us in the sacrament of reconciliation. As St Paul said:

> God in Christ was reconciling the world to himself, not holding men's faults against them, and he has entrusted to us the news that they are reconciled. So we are ambassadors for Christ; it is as though God were appealing through us, and the appeal that we make in Christ's name is: be reconciled to God. For our sake God made the sinless one into sin, so that in him we might become the goodness of God (2 Corinthians 5:19-21).

Every time we come to "the throne of grace and mercy" in the sacrament of reconciliation we are being freed from sin. What an amazing revelation! God's mercy transforms our sinful hearts and makes them the very goodness of God. In the words of St Bernard, "God's mercy becomes my merit". Truly, that is the amazing mercy of God. From being sinners turned in on ourselves, we become sharers in the very goodness of God, freed to go out in true love to others.

Sacrament of healing

The Church today teaches us that the sacrament of reconciliation is one of the sacraments of healing. We read in the Catechism:

> The Lord Jesus Christ, physician of souls and bodies, who forgave the sins of the paralytic and restored him to bodily health, has willed that his Church continue, in the power

of the Holy Spirit, his work of healing and salvation, even among her own members. This is the purpose of the two sacraments of healing: the sacrament of penance and the sacrament of anointing of the sick.[7]

Commenting on the healing effect of the sacrament of confession Carl Jung observed that there were "fewer neurotic Catholics" and concluded that Catholics owed this freedom to the sacrament of confession. How do we explain this effect of the sacrament today? In his introduction to the New Rite of Penance Blessed Paul VI said,

> In order that this sacrament of healing may truly achieve its purpose among Christ's faithful, it must take root in their whole lives and lead them to more fervent service of God and neighbour.[8]

Rooted in our whole life

Notice when the healing power of the sacrament begins to take effect – when it is "rooted" in our whole life. When we confess our sins with "a firm purpose of amendment", that is, with the determination, with God's help, to avoid the sin in the future. Even if we fail again, as so often we do, we keep "the purpose of amendment" alive in our hearts. We begin again. The first principle of spiritual growth is start again. The "purpose of amendment" keeps calling us back to the throne of mercy where we hear again the words God spoke to St Paul, "My grace is enough for you: my power is at its best in weakness" (2 Corinthians 12:9). It is a gross caricature to speak of Catholics going to confession and then being free to commit the same sins again. True sorrow for sin always includes that "purpose of amendment" which puts one's trust in God's mercy, despite all our weaknesses and sinfulness. The sacrament of confession is always a "sacrament of conversion" because it is only with a contrite spirit that we can approach "the throne of mercy". Blessed Paul VI describes conversion in this way:

---

7   Catechism of the Catholic Church, 1421
8   New Rite of Penance, 7

We can only approach the Kingdom of Christ by metanoia. This is a profound change of the whole person by which we begin to consider, judge, and arrange our life according to the holiness and love of God, made manifest in his Son in the last days and given to us in abundance. The genuineness of penance depends on this heartfelt contrition. For conversion should affect a person from within toward a progressively deeper enlightenment and an ever closer likeness to Christ.[9]

Each time we celebrate the sacrament we receive that "deeper enlightenment" and we grow in "an ever closer likeness to Christ". This is a gift of grace, a gift of mercy. As Cardinal Kasper writes, "Divine mercy grants sinners a period of grace and desires their conversion. Mercy is ultimately grace for conversion."[10] In fact, it is the gift which enables us to say "the mercy of God is my merit". In the sacrament of confession God takes away all our sins and, as the psalm says "crowns us with love and compassion" (Psalm 103:4). We would, therefore, be depriving ourselves of that wonderful richness of divine mercy if we didn't approach "the throne of grace and mercy" with confidence and gratitude. Every time we are touched by the mercy of God in the sacrament of confession, the grace of conversion is increased within our hearts and we grow in "that ever closer likeness to Christ". The great blessing that Christ has left to us poor sinners is that we have free access to the "throne of mercy" whenever we wish to receive the mercy of God in the sacrament of confession.

The wound of sin

What precisely does the sacrament heal? Blessed Paul VI answered that question in this way:

---

9   *Ibid*, 6
10 Cardinal Walter Kasper, *Mercy: The Essence of the Gospel and the Key to Christian Life*, Paulist Press, New York, 2014, p.54

Just as the wound of sin is varied and multiple in the life of individuals and of a community, so the healing which penance provides is varied.[11]

In celebrating the sacrament of confession our sins are forgiven but also, the "wounds of our sins" are healed.

In the Catechism of the Catholic Church we have this helpful definition of sin:

Sin is an offence against reason, truth and right conscience; it is failure in genuine love of God and neighbour caused by a perverse attachment to certain goods. It wounds the nature of man and injures human solidarity. It has been defined as "an utterance, a deed or a desire contrary to eternal life."[12]

In the first place, sin must be seen as an irrational act, "an offence against reason". It is contrary to our very nature, to our dignity as rational creatures whom God "has chosen for their own sake", to act in a totally selfish way. The Second Vatican Council said,

The Lord Jesus, when praying to the Father "that they may all be one... even as we are one" (John 17:21-22), has opened up new horizons closed to human reason by indicating that there is a certain similarity between the union existing among the divine persons and the union of God's children in truth and love. It follows, then, that if human beings are the only creatures on earth that God has wanted for their own sake, they can fully discover their true selves only in sincere self-giving,[13]

Discovering our true selves

Notice that it is through "sincere self-giving" that we discover our true selves. God reveals himself to us in his sincere self-giving and,

---

11 New Rite of Penance, 7
12 Catechism of the Catholic Church para 1849
13 Constitution on the Church in the Modern World, 24

by our sincere self-giving, we discover our true selves as made in the image of God. Christ, who is the perfect image of God, gives himself totally to us in a supreme act of love. The sinful act, on the contrary, denies that "self-giving" opens the door to the discovery of our true selves. It wants to "find the true self" on its own terms, like Adam and Eve who wanted to be like God by taking for themselves the "forbidden fruit" and eating it (Genesis 3:4). That is why sin is an offence against God. It wants to be like God, not by self-giving but by self-seeking.

Sin seeks to convince us that self-seeking, putting ourselves and our own interests before every other consideration, is the road to self-discovery and self-fulfilment. Experience, however, shows that all self-seeking ends ultimately in emptiness, loneliness and isolation. Those who are always self-seeking will never discover their true selves. They cruelly deprive themselves of the joy of knowing their true dignity as sons and daughters of God. By refusing to be self-giving they refuse to be like God. They fail to actualise their deepest human power which is the power to love. In the words of St John Paul II we have "the power to express love: precisely that love in which the human person becomes a gift – and through this gift – fulfils the very meaning of his or her being and existence".[14]

Sin, because it is always self-seeking, prevents us from discovering our true selves and "fulfilling the very meaning of our being and existence". No wonder, therefore, that the Church teaches us today that sin is "an offence against reason".

Sin is also destructive of human relationships because "it wounds the nature of man and injures human solidarity". Sin can never be an innocent action without serious consequences. If I do something that hurts another person I commit a sin in my heart and I also inflict a wound in the other person's heart. As a result, I have a sin on my conscience and he or she has the wound of my sin in their hearts. That

---

14 St John Paul II, *Theology of the Body*, Pauline Press, Boston 2006, 15: 1

wound in their hearts will often manifest itself in the way they react unlovingly towards others. They may then be very sorry for their bad reaction; they may see their bad reaction as their sin, whereas in fact it is really the manifestation of their wound. What they need most of all is healing rather than forgiveness. Blessed Paul VI in the New Rite of the Sacrament of Penance identified the healing of these wounds as the grace of the sacrament. Let us remind ourselves of what he wrote:

> Just as the wound of sin is varied and multiple in the life of individuals and of a community, so the healing which penance provides is varied.[15]

The wound of sin is a new concept in our Catholic consciousness. We have always regarded sin as an offence against God which, of course, it is. But we haven't given enough attention to the wound that the sins of others can inflict on us or the wounds that we can inflict on others by our own sins against them. If we take the time to engage in a deeper examination of our conscience, asking ourselves "why did I react in that bad way?" we may begin to get in touch with a deep inner wound that has never yet healed. That inner wound may be the cause of some of our self-seeking attitudes in our relationship with others which rob us of the joy of self-giving, the joy of discovering our true selves. Through the sacrament of penance we receive God's pardon for our sinful self-seeking and we also receive healing for the inner wound that is often the cause of our self-seeking.

When we approach "the throne of mercy" in the sacrament of confession we receive the welcome that the prodigal son received from his father. God delights in forgiving us. It is how he loves to manifest his power as we say in the prayer at Mass on the Twenty-sixth Sunday of Year A:

> O God, who manifest your almighty power above all by pardoning and showing mercy, bestow, we pray, your grace

---

15 *Ibid*

abundantly upon us and make those hastening to attain your promises heirs to the treasures of heaven.

Having our sins forgiven, knowing in our hearts that we are at peace with God, is the gracious manifestation of God's mercy and love. Nothing brings a deeper peace to the contrite heart than the words "I absolve you from all your sins in the name of the Father, and of the Son and of the Holy Spirit. Go in peace." But although the guilt of my own sin is forgiven by the God of mercies, the wounds that my sins inflicted on others need to be healed. Now I may be at peace, but those who were wounded by my sins may be experiencing inner pain and a lack of peace. The Catechism makes clear that sin "wounds the nature of man and injures human solidarity". Sin disrupts human relationships. When I receive "pardon and peace" for my own sins I have the inner strength to reach out to those whom my sins may have hurt. I can say that little word that Pope Francis keeps reminding us to say in all our relationships: sorry. We should also pray for those who have been hurt by our own self-seeking and hurtful behaviour.

The Church speaks about the wounds of sin and presents the sacrament of reconciliation as a sacrament that brings healing for the multiple wounds of sin. This vision of the sacrament healing the wounded heart has not, as yet, found its proper place in the preaching and teaching on this sacrament. We have not yet become very familiar with the notion of "the wound of sin". Indeed, many otherwise fine books on the sacrament of reconciliation have simply ignored this concept. These books deal, often very extensively, with the history of the sacrament, the development of the doctrine of the sacrament, the pastoral practice and the new rites for celebrating the sacrament, but inexplicably they ignore what is at the heart of Blessed Paul VI's vision for the renewal of the sacrament, namely that the sacrament is the great means for the healing of the inner wound inflicted on us by our own sins and the sins of others.

In the sacrament of reconciliation we have the forgiveness of all our sins. Jesus, who said to every repentant sinner who came to him while he was still on earth, "your sins are forgiven" (cf Luke 5:20; Luke 7:48; Matthew 9:5; John 8:1-11) says exactly the same liberating words to us in the sacrament of reconciliation as the priest says, "I absolve you from all your sins in the name of the Father and of the Son and of the Holy Spirit." In this sacrament we meet Jesus, "the Lamb of God, who takes away the sins of the world". In the words of the Psalm, "As far as the east is from the west so far does he remove our sins" (Psalm 103:12). This sacrament is the concrete manifestation of God "crowning us with love and compassion" (Psalm 103:4) as he manifests his great mercy to each of us as individuals. Since we have open access to such a wonderful source of divine mercy and forgiveness it is surely very puzzling that we can, at times, live as if this sacrament is for others and not for ourselves. Sometimes people can live for years burdened with their past sins and never experience the joy of knowing that they are "precious in God's eyes" (Isaiah 43:4). Jesus' open invitation to us sinners is there all the time: "Come to me all you who... are overburdened and I will give you rest" (Matthew 11: 28). On parish missions I have noticed how the Lord gives special graces to people who haven't celebrated the sacrament of reconciliation for years and come to make their confession. They usually begin with words like, "oh, father, it must be years since I was last at confession and I really don't know what to say". After a moment or two of prayer, the Holy Spirit enlightens them and they bring all their past sins and burdens to the Lord who always gives them his rest and his peace through the forgiveness of all their sins. As they are about to leave the confessional they usually say something like "oh, father, thank you so much, I feel a great burden has been lifted off me".

People sometimes use the very colourful phrase "I was walking on air as I came out of the confessional" to describe that freeing from burdens and the gift of peace which they receive in the sacrament.

That is what the priest prays for as he says "through the ministry of the Church may God give you pardon and peace". Pardon is for our sins, peace is for the healing of the wounds of sin – the healing of all the hurt, inner pain, resentment and all the bitterness that is like a poison in the heart. In the past we tended to place all the emphasis on our need for pardon, on the forgiveness of our sins, and we neglected that other great grace of the sacrament which is the healing of the wound of sin. Pope Francis in one of his homilies describes very well how the God of mercy is at work in the sacrament of confession:

> God's patience has to call forth in us the courage to return to him, however many mistakes and sins there may be in our life… It is there, in the wounds of Jesus, that we are truly secure; there we encounter the boundless love of his heart. Thomas understood this. St Bernard goes on to ask: But what can I count on? My own merits? No, "My merit is God's mercy. I am by no means lacking merits as long as he is rich in mercy. If the mercies of the Lord are manifold, I too will abound in merits". This is important: the courage to trust in Jesus' mercy, to trust in his patience, to seek refuge in the wounds of his love.[16]

Inner healing in the sacrament of reconciliation

The wound of sin is an inner wound. The person is wounded in his or her self-acceptance and self-esteem. A wound in self-acceptance leads to self-rejection. This can be a very deep inner wound which makes it very difficult for the person to "make the gift of self" in love to anyone. If self has been rejected there is no self at home to be offered to others! As we saw above, "we can discover our true selves only in sincere self-giving". While a person is burdened with self-rejection he or she can never make that sincere gift of self and never discover their true selves. But, once we open our hearts to the mercy of God, there is healing for that wound of self-rejection.

---

16 Homily on Divine Mercy Sunday, April 7, 2013

Self-rejection makes the person feel that nobody could ever love him or her. This wound of self-rejection is often the root cause of the person's "sinful reactions" in many situations. Self-rejection makes it impossible for the person to love self. Consequently the person will really struggle with the words of Jesus that we should "love our neighbour as ourselves". I can only love my neighbour with the same love that I have for myself. If I have no love for myself, how can I love my neighbour? St John Paul II in a wonderful teaching reminded us that without love life becomes meaningless:

> Humans cannot live without love. They remain a being that is incomprehensible for themselves; their lives are senseless if love is not revealed to them, if they do not encounter love, if they do not experience it and make it their own, if they do not participate in it.[17]

The experience of the gift of God's mercy and forgiveness that we receive in the celebration of the sacrament of reconciliation, heals those inner wounds in our hearts. Those wounds often rob us of joy by making it so difficult to reach out in true love to others. When those wounds are healed in the sacrament of confession we regain our power to make the sincere gift of self to others. And the big bonus, as we make that gift of self, we discover our true selves. This healing is the work of the Holy Spirit. As the Catechism says:

> Healing the wounds of sin, the Holy Spirit renews us interiorly through a spiritual transformation. He enlightens and strengthens us to live as "children of the light" through all that is good and right and true.[18]

The Catechism also reminds us that:

> Justification is not only the remission of sins, but also the sanctification and renewal of the interior man... Justification follows upon God's merciful initiative in

---

offering forgiveness. It reconciles men and women with God. It frees from the enslavement to sin, and it heals.[19]

When we come to the throne of God's mercy in the sacrament of reconciliation all our sins are forgiven and the wounds of our sins are healed.[20] We can leave the past to his great mercy, we can entrust the future to his divine providence, and we can live joyfully and gratefully in his presence in the present.

Personal spiritual exercise

Centre yourself; sitting upright; breathing rhythmically; clearing your mind of all preoccupations.

Bring yourself to bodily stillness.

Now say in your heart "I am coming to the throne of mercy".

Bring to the "throne" your sins and the wounds of sin within you.

Be still for some time in the presence of the God of mercy and compassion, receive his love and listen to his voice.

Now focus again on your breathing as you relax in God's presence.

And bring yourself gently back to the world.

This spiritual exercise will deepen your awareness of being in the presence of the God of mercy and make you more grateful for the mercy and forgiveness that God has for you in the sacrament of confession.

---

19 Catechism of the Catholic Church,1989-1990
20 For a more detailed discussion of inner healing see my books, *Healing In the Spirit*, and *The Healing Power of the Sacraments* published by Redemptorist Publications..

— Chapter Six —

Dining at the Table of Mercy

Jesus chose to recline at table in the homes of those whom the religious leaders of his time considered public sinners and renegades from the true religion. This was his very concrete and practical way of proclaiming the mercy of the heavenly Father. He didn't just talk about mercy; he showed people what mercy looked like in action.

St Luke records Jesus' first feast with sinners in the household of a tax collector by the name of Levi. Jesus saw Levi "sitting by the customs house, and said to him, 'Follow me'. And leaving everything he got up and followed him" (Luke 5:27). Levi had become a disciple of Jesus. He had given up his former way of life and his former occupation as a tax collector. Now he wants to honour the Lord who has given him this new life. St Luke says,

> Levi held a great reception in his house, and with them at table was a large gathering of tax collectors and others. The Pharisees and their scribes complained to his disciples and said, "Why do you eat and drink with tax collectors and sinners?" Jesus said to them in reply, "It is not those who are well who need the doctor, but the sick. I have not come to call the virtuous, but sinners to repentance" (Luke 5: 27-32).

In the eyes of the Pharisees, a large group of tax collectors was the most disreputable group one could imagine. And there was Jesus and his disciples at table with them! But, we could ask, what were the complaining Pharisees doing at that party? Eugene LaVerdiere observes:

> This would suggest that in some or even many of the Lukan communities there were those who thought themselves

righteous and who judged others as unrighteous. These Christian Pharisees were ready to be with Jesus and his disciples, but they objected to the presence of the tax collectors, whom they considered unrighteous.[1]

All are welcome at the Lord's table

Jesus made it very clear that all are welcome at his table, because at his table it is the mercy of God that is shared by all. Jesus invites each of us to take our place at the table of God's mercy and share a meal with him. As he serves us at the table of mercy he takes the bread and says to us, "Take it and eat... this is my body." Then he takes the chalice and giving thanks says to us, "Drink all of you from this... for this is my blood, the blood of the covenant, which is to be poured out for many for the forgiveness of sins" (Matthew 26: 20; 26:28). In this supreme act of love and mercy Jesus gives us the Eucharistic banquet of his body and blood, under the appearance of bread and wine, which is the Mass and which is celebrated every day in the Catholic churches throughout the world. Contemplating this mystery St Alphonsus Liguori exclaimed:

> If anything could shake my faith in the Eucharist it would not be the doubt as to how bread and wine could become flesh... because I should answer that God can do everything; but if I ask myself how could he love us so much as to make himself our food, I can only answer that this is a mystery of faith above my comprehension, and that the love of Jesus cannot be understood.[2]

As we take our place at the table of mercy, each time we participate in the celebration of the Mass, we know the truth of Pope Francis' teaching:

---

1   Eugene LaVerdiere, *Dining in the Kingdom of God: The Origins of the Eucharist in the Gospel of Luke*, Liturgical Training Publications, Chicago, 1994, p. 43
2   St Alphonsus de Liguori , *The Holy Eucharist*, Centenary Edition 1887, p.239

Mercy is the very foundation of the Church's life. All of her pastoral activity should be caught up in the tenderness she makes present to believers; nothing in her preaching and in her witness to the world can be lacking in mercy. The Church's very credibility is seen in how she shows merciful and compassionate love. The Church has an endless desire to show mercy. Perhaps we have long since forgotten how to show mercy and live the way of mercy.[3]

We can look at the wonderful mystery of the Mass from many points of view.[4] In these reflections I want to focus specifically on how the Mass is, for us Catholics, the greatest manifestation of God's mercy. As Pope Francis says, "Mercy is the very foundation of the Church's life" and, in the words of St John Paul II, "The Church draws her life from the Eucharist". In the very first paragraph of his last great encyclical on The Eucharist, he wrote:

> The Church draws her life from the Eucharist. This truth does not simply express a daily experience of faith, but recapitulates the heart of the mystery of the Church. In a variety of ways she joyfully experiences the constant fulfilment of the promise: "Lo, I am with you always, to the close of the age" (Matthew 28:20), but in the Holy Eucharist, through the changing of bread and wine into the body and blood of the Lord, she rejoices in this presence with unique intensity. Ever since Pentecost, when the Church, the People of the New Covenant, began her pilgrim journey towards her heavenly homeland, the Divine Sacrament has continued to mark the passing of her days, filling them with confident hope.[5]

---

3 Pope Francis, Bull of Indiction of the Extraordinary Jubilee Year of Mercy, 10
4 For a detailed examination of what we are doing when we gather to celebrate Mass see my book, *Going to Mass: Becoming the Eucharist we Celebrate*, published by Redemptorist Publications 2014
5 St John Paul II, Encyclical on the Eucharist, 1

Mercy is the foundation of the Church

Mercy is the foundation of the life of the Church and the Church draws her life from the Eucharist. There is, therefore, an inseparable bond between the mercy of God and the Eucharist. When we come to celebrate Mass we are, in fact, celebrating the mystery, the sacrament of God's mercy. Jesus said, "God loved the world so much that he gave his only Son, so that everyone who believes in him may not be lost but may have eternal life" (John 3:16). And he tells us that he gives us this eternal life through the Eucharist. He says, "Anyone who does eat my flesh and drink my blood has eternal life, and I shall raise him up on the last day" (John 6:54). St Ignatius of Antioch, one of the early Apostolic Fathers of the Church, who was martyred around the year 108 AD, called the Eucharist:

> The medicine of immortality, the antidote to death and the food that makes us live for ever in Jesus Christ.[6]

We all hold, deep in our hearts, these wonderful truths about the mystery we are celebrating when we participate in the Mass. Sometimes, however, routine can rob us of that eucharistic amazement which enables us, at each celebration, to enter more deeply into the mystery of this infinite manifestation of God's great mercy. To retain this eucharistic amazement we have to reflect regularly on what we are doing when we go to Mass.

The eucharistic community

The first thing we do is we come together as a community, as the sacred assembly of God's people. Indeed our very word church, long before it was applied to the building in which we celebrate, was applied to the community who assembled to celebrate. The primary meaning of the word church is the assembly of the people. So, when I say I am going to church I am saying that I am entering into the assembly of the people who have gathered to celebrate the

---

6   Catechism of the Catholic Church, 1405

wonderful mystery of the Lord's Supper. When we gather for this celebration, our very first thoughts turn to the mercy of God. We join in our great invocation for mercy and we say, "Lord, have mercy; Christ, have mercy; Lord, have mercy." This appeal to the Lord for mercy sets the tone of everything else we do during the celebration of the Mass. As we join in praying the great Gloria we return several times to reminding Jesus that he brings us the mercy of the Father: "Lord God, Lamb of God, Son of the Father, you take away the sins of the world have mercy on us;... you are seated at the right hand of the Father, have mercy on us." We shout out that appeal to Jesus with total confidence because we believe that he is, as Pope Francis says, "the face of the Father's mercy". We come back to this prayer to the Lamb of God just before receiving Holy Communion when we say twice, "Lamb of God, you take away the sins of the world, have mercy on us" and then "grant us peace". We begin our Mass with the appeal to Jesus for his mercy and then, just before we receive him into our hearts in Holy Communion, we again appeal for his mercy. In one of the Sunday prayers at Mass the whole community is reminded that mercy is the manifestation of God's power:

> O God, who manifest your almighty power above all by pardoning and showing mercy, bestow, we pray, your grace abundantly upon us and make those hastening to attain your promises heirs to the treasures of heaven, through our Lord Jesus Christ.[7]

These constantly repeated prayers and songs for the mercy of God should leave us in no doubt that the great mystery of the Mass is truly the manifestation of God the Father's mercy for his children and the manifestation of the mercy of Jesus Christ who has left us such a wonderful sacrament for celebrating mercy. St John Paul II brings out this great truth in this way:

---

7   Prayer for the Mass on the Twenty-sixth Sunday of Year A.

When the Church celebrates the Eucharist, the memorial of her Lord's death and resurrection, this central event of salvation becomes really present and "the work of our redemption is carried out". This sacrifice is so decisive for the salvation of the human race that Jesus Christ offered it and returned to the Father only after he had left us a means of sharing in it as if we had been present there.[8]

We are present at the great work of our Redemption as we celebrate the mystery of the Mass. We are at the very table of God's mercy for us sinners. Let us reflect now on what we are doing when we enter into the mystery of the Mass. We are engaging in four different actions: we listen, we respond, we offer and we receive.

We listen

We listen to the word of God being proclaimed. Every Sunday we hear God speaking to us through readings from the Old and the New Testaments. The Second Vatican Council alerts us to what is happening when the scriptures are being proclaimed:

In the sacred books the Father who is in heaven comes lovingly to meet his children and talks with them. And such is the force and the power of the word of God that it can serve the Church as her support and vigour, and the children of the Church as strength for their faith, food for their soul, and a pure and lasting fount of spiritual life.[9]

God our Father is speaking lovingly to us as we sit at the table of mercy. His words are life-giving and full of mercy. As we receive them into our hearts our faith is renewed, our hope in life and in God is enlivened, and our love of God and our neighbour is inflamed. But so often we struggle to pay attention. As Jesus said to his sleeping disciples in the garden of Gethsemane during his agony, he surely

---

8   St John Paul II, Encyclical on the Eucharist, 11
9   Constitution on Divine Revelation 21

often says to us as we seem to fall asleep during the proclamation of the word of God, "the spirit is willing but the flesh is weak" (Matthew 26:41). Each time we become aware that we haven't really been listening attentively we are making progress. We need the special grace of the Holy Spirit to listen and welcome the word that God speaks to us. St Jerome said, "We cannot come to an understanding of Scripture without the assistance of the Holy Spirit who inspired it".[10] As we allow the Holy Spirit to open our hearts we will begin to hear the words of scripture in a new way. St Paul tells us that "the word of God is something alive and active" (Hebrews 4:12). It is not a word from the past, about some situation in the past. It is spoken to us in the present. But without faith we will not be able to hear it as a personal word. St Thomas Aquinas said:

> The letter even of the Gospel would kill were there not the inward grace of healing faith.[11]

As the Gospel is proclaimed, Jesus himself is speaking directly to us. He is inviting us to begin afresh and to live "on every word that comes from the mouth of God" (Matthew 4:4). Indeed he invites us to enter into his word and make our home in it:

> If you make my word your home
> you will indeed be my disciples,
> you will learn the truth
> and the truth will make you free (John 8:31).

This invitation to make our home in Christ's word is an invitation to be at home in the mercy of God. Christ's word is creative and life-giving. When many of his followers walked away from Jesus because they could not accept what he said about his body and blood being our spiritual food and drink, Jesus said to the Twelve: "What about you, do you want to go away too?" Simon Peter answered, "Lord, to whom shall we go? You have the message of eternal life,

---

10 Cf. Benedict XVI, Verbum Domini, Post-Synodal Exhortation on the Word of God, 2010, para 16
11 St Thomas Aquinas, Summa Theologica, 1a – IIae, q. 106, art 2

and we believe, we know that you are the Holy One of God" (John 6:69). Peter is professing his belief that the word of Christ opens the door to eternal life to those who receive it and believe it. At each Mass we are invited afresh to hear the word of God, to receive it into our hearts, "to make our home in it". This is an essential part of our celebration of the holy Mass.

That is why Benedict XVI wrote,

> From the two tables of the word of God and the Body of Christ, the Church receives and gives to the faithful the bread of life. Consequently it must constantly be kept in mind that the word of God, read and proclaimed in the Church in the liturgy, leads to the Eucharist as to its own connatural end.[12]

Listening attentively to the word of God proclaimed during the first part of the Mass, that we call the liturgy of the Word, is an integral part of our Eucharistic celebration and a necessary preparation of our minds and hearts for entering more deeply into the mystery of the Mass. As Benedict XVI said, "Word and Eucharist are so deeply bound together that we cannot understand one without the other."[13]

We respond

When somebody speaks words of encouragement to us we respond with gratitude. When the person speaking those words of encouragement to us is God himself we respond with even greater enthusiasm and gratitude. We try to put our whole hearts into our responses. For instance, when we are invited to say together the Gloria at Mass, consider the enthusiastic words we use: "We praise you, we bless you, we adore you, we glorify you, we give you thanks for your great glory." These fervent words of praise, directed to the heart of Jesus, open our hearts to receive the great gift that the Lord always wants to give, the gift of his mercy. And so, we

---

12 Benedict XVI, *Sacramentum Caritatis: Post Synodal Exhortation on the Eucharist*, 44
13 Benedict XVI, Verbum Domini, Post-Synodal Exhortation on the Word of God, 2010, para 55

are emboldened to appeal to the Lord with great confidence: "Lord God, Lamb of God, Son of the Father, you take away the sins of the world, have mercy on us; you take away the sins of the world, receive our prayer; you are seated at the right hand of the Father, have mercy on us. For you alone are the Holy One… "

Every time we respond to the word of God in Mass and ask for his mercy, his forgiveness and his protection, we should try to make these prayers with the greatest confidence. When we ask him for mercy, his heart rejoices, because his love for us is so great that he actually died on the Cross for our redemption. And before he died he gave us the great sacrament, the mystery of the Mass, to ensure that we can participate in his great act of love… As St John Paul II said,

> This sacrifice is so decisive for the salvation of the human race that Jesus Christ offered it and returned to the Father only after he had left us a means of sharing in it as if we had been present there.[14]

As we celebrate Mass we are sharing, sacramentally, in Christ's great sacrifice for our salvation. It is truly the mystery of faith. Benedict XVI expresses this mystery well:

> In the most blessed Eucharist is contained the entire spiritual wealth of the Church, namely Christ himself our Pasch and our living bread, who gives life to humanity through his flesh – that flesh which is given life and gives life by the Holy Spirit.[15]

Our participation in the celebration of the mystery of the Mass should always be a time of great joy and inner peace because we know we are at the table of God's mercy where Jesus, the Lamb of God, takes away all our sins and the mercy of God becomes our merit.

---

14 St John Paul II, *Encyclical on the Eucharist*, 11
15 Benedict XVI, *Sacramentum Caritatis*, 16

We offer

Having listened attentively to God's word and responded with joy and gratitude we are now ready to offer God our gifts. Our gifts of bread and wine are brought to the altar and the priest offers them to God with the beautiful prayer:

> Blessed are you, Lord God of all creation, for through your goodness we have received the bread we offer you: fruit of the earth and work of human hands, it will become for us the bread of life.

Offering God our gifts of bread and wine is one of the most beautiful moments of the celebration of Mass and we have constantly to remind ourselves of its significance. Through our gifts we are saying to God that we love him with our whole heart. A gift is the universal symbol of love. It speaks a message of love to the one to whom it is given. So, for instance, when you give a close friend a gift, a box of chocolates or a bottle of wine, your gift is saying "I love you" and not "you love chocolates or wine"! The gift represents your whole attitude to your friend. Similarly, the gifts we offer to God at Mass represent our whole attitude to God. They represent ourselves. It is, therefore, the gift of our very selves that we are offering to God. This is a moment of great spiritual significance, leading to a wonderful spiritual transformation for us. Our gifts represent our whole being, everything about us: all the good and all the bad; all the virtues and all the vices; all the holiness and all the sinfulness. And God, who is graciousness itself, gratefully receives our gifts and receives us too.

As we stand before God offering him the gift of ourselves, God who is "the God of mercies", receives us into the embrace of his merciful love and assures us of his acceptance. At this moment we are encountering our God in faith, not in feeling or sentiment; and we believe that God accepts us because, he says to us, "you are precious in my eyes" (Isaiah 43:10); we believe what we say when we say to God in Mass, "You have held us worthy to be in your presence and serve you"; and, most of all, we believe that the sign that we are truly one with Christ our Lord will be the transformation of the bread and wine, that represent ourselves and our love of God, into the body and blood of Christ. When the priest offers the bread and wine to God he then imposes his hands over our gift and prays:

> Therefore, O Lord, we humbly implore you: by the same Spirit graciously make holy these gifts we have brought to you for consecration, that they may become the Body and Blood of Your Son our Lord Jesus Christ, at whose command we celebrate these mysteries.[16]

That consecration happens through the power of the Holy Spirit. All we can say in response is: "The mystery of faith!" But notice what the mystery of faith truly is: the bread and wine that represent us before God have now become for us the very body and blood of Christ. As our gifts of bread and wine are changed by the power of the Holy Spirit, we too are changed utterly by the same Holy Spirit. Speaking at his first World Youth Day in Cologne in August 2005, Benedict XVI said to a million young people:

> The body and blood of Christ are given to us so that we ourselves will be transformed in our turn. We are to become the body of Christ, his own flesh and blood. We all eat one bread, and this means that we ourselves become one. In this way adoration becomes union. God no longer simply stands before us as the One who is totally Other. He is within us, and we are in him. His dynamic enters into us and then seeks to spread upwards to others until it fills the world, so that his love can truly become the dominant measure of the world.[17]

We have then the miracle of two transformations as we celebrate Mass: the miracle of the transformation of our gifts of bread and wine into the body and blood of Christ and the mystery of our

---

16   Eucharistic Prayer 3
17   Accessed via internet.

transformation into the body of Christ in this world. After our prayer of Consecration we pray: "Grant that we who are nourished by the Body and Blood of your Son and filled with his Holy Spirit may become one body, one spirit in Christ".[18] Fr Cantalamessa explains this twofold transformation in this way:

> There are two bodies of Christ on the altar: his real body (the body "born of the Virgin Mary", risen and ascended into heaven) and his mystic body, the Church. Thus, his real body is really present and his mystic body is mystically present, "mystically" meaning in virtue of its inseparable union with the Head. There is no confusion and no division between the two presences which are distinct.[19]

The mystery of faith, then, is twofold. The bread and wine are changed into the body and blood of Christ and we too are transformed and become "one body, one Spirit in Christ". The body of Christ becomes truly present under the appearance of the bread and wine on the altar and, at the same time, the body of Christ becomes mystically present in the disciples around the altar. That is the profound mystery of our faith involving both Christ and us. The new Catechism of the Catholic Church teaches the depth of the mystery of faith by quoting the words of St Augustine:

> If you are the body and members of Christ, then it is your sacrament that is placed on the table of the Lord; it is your sacrament that you receive. To that which you respond, "Amen" ("yes, it is true") and by responding to it you assent to it. For you hear the word, "the Body of Christ" and respond "Amen". Be then a member of the body of Christ so that your Amen may be true.[20]

What mercy the Lord shows us. We acknowledge that we are sinners. We confess our sins to God and to each other as we begin Mass with the words, "I confess to almighty God and to you my brothers and

---

18 Eucharistic Prayer 3
19 Raniero Cantalamessa, *The Eucharist*, Liturgical Press, Collegeville, 1995, p.21
20 St Augustine cited in The Catechism of the Catholic Church, 1396

sisters, that I have greatly sinned, in my thoughts and in my words, in what I have done and in what I have failed to do, through my fault, through my fault, through my most grievous fault." I am not trying to make excuses, nor am I living in denial. In this confession I lift up my hands to God and admit that I am a sinner in need of his forgiveness. Then God takes over. He forgives all my sins and the sins of each person at Mass with me: he fills us afresh with his Holy Spirit and we become "one body, one Spirit in Christ". God's merciful love transforms our spiritual lives into Christ's life in this world. Each of us can now say with St Paul, "I live now, not with my own life but with the life of Christ who loved me and who sacrificed himself for my sake" (Galatians 2:20).

In our faith in God's transforming love we have to resist all doubt. When Jesus says to us in the sacrament of confession "your sins are forgiven", they are forgiven; when our gifts of bread and wine are transformed into the body and blood of Christ we too are transformed despite all our sinful weaknesses. Recall the difficulties Fr Eugene, whom we met in the first chapter, had when he believed that each person in his parish was precious in God's sight, but didn't believe he was precious to God also. At Mass each person, who has opened his or her heart to God, becomes "one body, one spirit, in Christ". And that includes me and it includes you! We have to resist the temptation that whispers that this transformation only happens to the 'holy ones'. Jesus himself said, "It is not the healthy who need the doctor, but the sick. I did not come to call the virtuous, but sinners" (Mark 2:17). If we want to be called by Christ for this transformation into his body in this world we take our place with the sinners. When I can sincerely pray "Lord, have mercy on me a sinner" I am ready for this spiritual transformation.

We maintain a healthy spiritual balance in the Mass, between our awareness of being sinners, in need of God's mercy, and our faith that through the power of the Holy Spirit we become the body of Christ in the world. We see this balance well expressed in the words we say just before we receive Holy Communion: "Lord, I am not worthy that you should enter under my roof but only say the word and my soul shall be healed". The perfect balance. I am worthy, not because I am virtuous but because God has said the word that heals and forgives, the word "that counts me worthy to be in his presence". And when I come forward to receive Holy Communion I am not just receiving Christ but Christ is receiving me. If I feel that I have not prepared myself well, that I have been too distracted throughout the Mass, I must now let Christ take over. As St John Paul II wrote:

> Incorporation into Christ, which is brought about by baptism, is constantly renewed and consolidated by sharing in the Eucharistic Sacrifice, especially by that full sharing which takes place in sacramental communion. We can say not only that each of us receives Christ, but also that Christ receives each of us. He enters into friendship with us: "You are my friends" (John 15:14). Indeed, it is because of him that we have life: "He who eats me will live because of me" (John 6:57). Eucharistic communion brings about in a sublime way the mutual "abiding" of Christ and each of his followers: "Abide in me, and I in you" (John 15:4).[21]

That is the miracle and the mystery of Christ's love for us. He takes away all our sins, fills us with his own Spirit and makes us members of his own body in this world. We become the Eucharist we celebrate.

We receive

Christ enters our hearts in Holy Communion so to transform us that we become his body in this world. In the words of St Leo the Great, "Our partaking of the Body and Blood of Christ tends only to make us become what we eat".[22] The living bread that we eat in Holy Communion is not transformed into our body, rather we are transformed into Christ's body. St Augustine expressed this amazing truth in this way:

---

21 St John Paul II, Encyclical on the Eucharist, 22
22 St Leo the Great, Sermon 12 on the Passion. Cit. by Raniero Cantalamessa, *The Eucharist*, Collegeville, 1995, p.39

He who suffered for us has entrusted to us in this Sacrament his body and blood, which indeed he has even made us. For we have been made his body, and by his mercy, we are that which we receive.[23]

Our Holy Communion, therefore, is much more than receiving Christ into our hearts, wonderful though that is. It is Christ receiving us so completely into his heart that we become one Spirit with him. Each time we receive Holy Communion we become more deeply one with Christ. The words of St Paul are realised: "The human race has nothing to boast about to God, but you, God has made members of Christ Jesus and by God's doing he has become our wisdom, and our virtue, and our holiness, and our freedom" (1 Corinthians 1:30). Christ said, "I have come that they may have life and have it to the full" (John 10:10). When we receive Christ in Holy Communion he fills us with his abundant life. His life becomes our life; his holiness becomes our holiness; his virtue becomes our virtue. In a very special way we can say with St Bernard in our Holy Communion, "the mercy of God becomes my merit". In this intimate communion with Christ we let go of all our worries and doubts, our fears and guilt, our sins and failures.

It is as a member of the family of God that we receive Holy Communion. That is why in the Mass, just before we receive Holy Communion, we remind ourselves that God is our loving Father and we are his children as we pray The Lord's Prayer. It is a beautiful prayer of praise and petition. We praise God for his great glory as we say "hallowed be thy name". The great African Father of the Church, Tertullian, writing in the third century said,

> When we say "hallowed be thy name", we ask that it should be hallowed in us, who are in him; but also in others whom God's grace still awaits, that we may obey the precept that

---

23 Quoted in James T. O'Connor, *The Hidden Manna: Theology of the Eucharist*, Ignatius Press, San Francisco,1988, p.61

obliges us to pray for everyone, even our enemies. That is why we do not say expressly hallowed be thy name "in us", for we ask that it be so in all men.[24]

When we pray "hallowed be thy name", we are saying "save your people, Lord". The petition "hallowed be thy name" in The Lord's Prayer sums up everything that Jesus wants the Father to do for us. Jesus wants the Father to save us, to sanctify us, to protect us from all evil. The grace that I am asking for myself in the Lord's Prayer I am also asking for everyone, even those who offend me or who have become my enemies. We say "our Father" not "my Father". We need Christ's redemption before we can truly speak the word 'our'. In God's presence, who am I including in that little word 'our'? Or, am I excluding anyone from being included in that word 'our'? Benedict XVI wrote:

> When we say the word *our*, we say "Yes" to the living Church in which the Lord wanted to gather his new family. In this sense the Our Father is at once fully personal and a thoroughly ecclesial prayer. In praying the Our Father, we pray totally with our own heart, but at the same time we pray in communion with the whole family of God, with the living and the dead, with people of all conditions, cultures, and races. The Our Father overcomes all boundaries and makes us one family.[25]

In the Mass we stand before God with everyone in our life, even though some of them may have become our enemies. In the Mass we have the grace to include them all in the Our Father. When we say "*our*" we are speaking on their behalf as well. Of course, we had the golden opportunity to offer the pain of broken relationships to God as we presented our gifts at the altar. If we refused to offer the conflict and the hurt and pain of the conflict to God at the Offertory, then we should not be too surprised if we find it difficult to include

---

24 Catechism of the Catholic Church, 2814
25 Benedict XVI, *Jesus of Nazareth*, Bloomsbury, London 2007, p.141

"the enemies" in the "*our*" with which we address the Father. Before Jesus gave us the Our Father as our great Christian family prayer he said to us,

> I say this to you: love your enemies and pray for those who persecute you; in this way you will be sons of your Father in heaven, for he causes his sun to rise on bad men as well as good, and his rain to fall on honest and dishonest men alike. For if you love those who love you, what right have you to claim any credit? Even the tax collectors do as much, do they not?... You must therefore be perfect just as your heavenly Father is perfect (Matthew 5: 44-48).

We can love our enemies with that love of the Father because, as St Paul says, "the love of God has been poured into our hearts by the Holy Spirit which has been given us" (Romans 5:5).

Receiving the mercy of God during our celebration of the Mass gives us the strength to offer that same mercy to those who have offended us. So we say, "Forgive us our offences as we forgive those who offend us." This is how we become the Eucharist we celebrate. The sacrament of the Mass is the great sacrament of God's mercy. Without our willingness to share that mercy with everyone we will be resisting becoming the Eucharist we celebrate. Just as in the Eucharist Jesus gives himself freely to us in his mercy and love so we too try to give ourselves to others in mercy and love. At times we may have to struggle with making this gift to someone who has really upset us. But we should resist the urge not to forgive from the heart and pray for the grace to forgive. Jesus says to us, "I tell you therefore: everything you ask and pray for, believe that you have it already, and it will be yours. And when you stand in prayer, forgive whatever you have against anybody, so that your Father in heaven may forgive your failings too" (Mark 11:25). Jesus puts forgiveness at the very centre of our relationship with God the Father. The mercy we receive from the Father for our own sins must be shared with those who sin against us. Recall the parable of the servant who received the remission of an enormous debt and then refused to remit the very small debt of a fellow servant (see Chapter Four).

Filled with God's love and with his Spirit in the celebration of the holy Eucharist, we are moved to offer to others what God has given us, namely unconditional forgiveness. Forgiveness is the work of the Spirit. Christ's forgiveness comes to us in the Spirit and our forgiveness of others goes to them in the Spirit. St Paul says: "Since the Spirit is our life, let us be directed by the Spirit" (Galatians 5:25). For the Christian, forgiveness is a mark of our reconciliation with God. But forgiveness does not require social reconciliation between offender and victim, since it can be offered to the unrepentant as much as the repentant [26]. In Mass we are invited to heal the stress, caused by "the wounds of sin" inflicted by others, through forgiveness and offering the sign of peace. This is the surest way of healing the broken heart.

In our celebration of the Mass we receive the grace to forgive from the heart as we say the Lord's Prayer. This grace heals the broken heart and brings great peace and joy. If you have a deep hurt in your life you should always bring it to Mass, offer it to God, and open your heart to receive the healing that comes through forgiveness. You will certainly receive that healing if you are willing to forgive. And, to encourage yourself to forgive, you could remind yourself frequently that by harbouring bitterness and resentment you are hurting only yourself.

Dining at the table of the Lord's mercy as we celebrate the Holy Eucharist is the most solemn moment in the life of each Christian. As the Catechism of the Catholic Church teaches us:

> The Eucharist is the "source and summit of the Christian life". The other sacraments, and indeed all ecclesiastical ministries and works of the apostolate, are bound up with

---

26 For a detailed study of the health benefits of forgiving from the heart see *Finding Forgiveness* by Jim McManus C.Ss.R. and Dr Stephanie Thornton published by Redemptorist Publications 2008.

the Eucharist and are orientated to it. For in the blessed Eucharist is contained the whole spiritual good of the Church, namely Christ himself, our Pasch.[27]

We are, therefore, at the "summit of our Christian life" during the celebration of the Mass. We experience the mercy and the holiness, the forgiveness and the love of God our Father, his great gifts of redemption, which he asks us to share with all our brothers and sisters. Our hearts are full of gratitude and amazement as we come forward to receive Christ in Holy Communion. In the words of Benedict XVI, "The Eucharist draws us into Jesus' act of self-oblation. More than just statically receiving the incarnate Word, we enter into the very dynamic of his self-giving."[28] It is in and through Christ's self-giving that we now have the power to make the gift of self. And, as we make that gift of self we become the Eucharist we celebrate.

Pope Francis invites us to ponder this great Eucharistic mystery:

> The Eucharist is the sacrament of communion that brings us out of our individualism so that we can follow him together, living out our faith in him. Therefore we should ask ourselves before the Lord: how do I live the Eucharist? Do I live it anonymously or as a moment of true communion with the Lord, and also with all the brothers and sisters who share the same banquet?[29]

---

27 Catechism of the Catholic Church, 1324
28 Benedict XVI, *Sacramentum Caritatis*, 11
29 Pope Francis, *Homily for the Solemnity of Corpus Christi*, Thursday 30 May 2013

Personal spiritual exercise

Centre yourself; sitting upright; breathing rhythmically; clearing your mind of all preoccupations.

Bring yourself to bodily stillness.

Now say in your heart, "At Mass I sit with all my brothers and sisters at the table of God's mercy".

Bring to the table of mercy anyone you have trouble with and ask God to bless them.

Be still for some time in the presence of the God of mercy and compassion and receive his love.

Now focus again on your breathing as you relax in God's presence.

And bring yourself gently back to the world.

This spiritual exercise will deepen your awareness of being in the presence of the God of mercy and make you more grateful for the mercy and forgiveness you receive in the holy Eucharist.

— Chapter Seven —

Mercy: the healing of the whole person

The encounter with Jesus in the celebration of the sacraments, or in our personal prayer, is an experience of the healing of the whole person in body, mind and spirit. How often people describe the experience of mercy in the sacrament of reconciliation as "a great burden has been lifted off me". The forgiveness of sins, and the healing of the wounds of sin in our lives, are often accompanied by this physical sense of being freed from a great burden that has weighted us down in mind and heart and spirit. Of course, this is precisely what Jesus promises: "Come to me, all you who labour and are overburdened and I will give you rest" (Matthew 11:28). In this chapter I want to discuss with you this experience of mercy in the sacrament of the anointing of the sick.

St James, speaking about how the Church brings the experience of God's mercy to the sick, wrote:

> If one of you is ill, he should send for the elders of the church, and they must anoint him with oil in the name of the Lord and pray over him. The prayer of faith will save the sick person and the Lord will raise him up again; and if he has committed any sins, he will be forgiven (James 5:14-15).

In the Catholic Church we recognise this anointing in the name of the Lord as "the sacrament of the sick".

A sacrament is an intimate, personal encounter with the risen Lord who is the "face of the Father's mercy"[1]. As St Leo the Great said, "The visible presence of the Redeemer passed over into the sacraments."[2] It is Jesus, the very embodiment of the mercy of God, whom the sick person meets when he or she receives the sacrament of the sick. This sacrament should always be celebrated in a very reverent way. The sick person, at times, has to be encouraged to open his or her whole life in great trust to the Lord who comes to embrace him or her with the Father's great mercy. As Pope Francis says, "Everything in Jesus speaks of mercy. Nothing in him is devoid of compassion."[3] We believe that Jesus meets the sick person in love and forgiveness and with the gift of "life to the full' (John 10:10). The Vatican Council tells us that in this sacrament priests "by the anointing of the sick, relieve those who are ill".[4]

Personal story

When I was anointing my mother in her final illness I asked her how she was feeling about herself in her sickness and she said, "I am ready to go the moment God calls me". She knew that she was very ill and close to her end in this world. Her thoughts were happily fixed on eternity. The sacrament of anointing for her was an experience of the mercy of God bringing great integration and healing to her whole life. She was filled with deep peace as she waited for her call to go to the Father's house. Two of the family sat with her day and night in her hospital room. Each day I brought them Holy Communion and my mother received with great joy and reverence. Two days before she died she went into a coma and couldn't open her mouth, even for a drop of water. Nevertheless, I said I would bring Holy Communion to my brother and sister, who were sitting with her. As she would not be able to receive I would bless her with the Blessed Sacrament. But as I entered her room, her eyes opened widely and they were shining like the sun. I said

---

1   Pope Francis, Bull of Indiction of Jubilee Year of Mercy, 1
2   Office of Readings, Friday after the Ascension
3   *Ibid*, 8
4   Life of Priests, 5

to my sister, "she has recognised the Lord's coming". We said the prayers in preparation for Holy Communion and then I held up the sacred host and said, "Mammy, the Body of Christ" and she opened her mouth and received Holy Communion. Then she went back into her coma. Two days later, just before she died, she opened her eyes once more, looked for a long time at each of us, her six sons and two daughters around her bed, her eyes communicating that she was happy we were all there, and then for the last time in this world she closed her eyes, went to sleep and peacefully died as we were praying. This precious death-bed experience of anointing my mother and bringing her Holy Communion as viaticum taught me more about the sacraments than anything I had ever read. This was truly her final encounter on this earth with the Lord of mercy and we were greatly blessed as we shared her last moments. We knew the Lord was present.

The Catechism of the Catholic Church defines viaticum in this way:

> In addition to the anointing of the sick, the Church offers those who are about to leave this life the Eucharist as viaticum. Communion in the body and blood of Christ, received at this moment of "passing over" to the Father, has a particular significance and importance. It is the seed of eternal life and the power of the resurrection, according to the words of the Lord: "He who eats my flesh and drinks my blood has eternal life, and I will raise him up at the last day. The sacrament of Christ once dead and now risen, the Eucharist is here the sacrament of passing over from death to life, from this world to the Father."[5]

Thus, just as the sacraments of baptism, confirmation, and the Eucharist form a unity called "the sacraments of Christian initiation", so too it can be said that penance, the anointing of the sick and the Eucharist as viaticum constitute at the end of Christian life

---

5   Catechism of the Catholic Church,1524

"the sacraments that prepare for our heavenly homeland", or the sacraments that complete the earthly pilgrimage.[6]

When my mother said to me "I am ready to go the moment God calls me" I knew that she had almost "completed her earthly pilgrimage". The experience of her coming out of the coma to receive Holy Communion as her viaticum has stayed with me as a grace-filled reminder that Christ, the very mercy of God, is faithful, and in the sacrament of anointing and in the Holy Eucharist as viaticum, he came to take my mother to the Father's house "the moment the Father called her". The grace of the happy death is the most wonderful manifestation of the mercy of God the Father. He created her and now he called her to himself.

Fruits of the sacrament of anointing

What are the fruits of this personal encounter with Jesus in the sacrament of anointing? In the Rite of Anointing we are told the effect of the sacrament:

> This sacrament gives the grace of the Holy Spirit to those who are sick: by this grace the whole person is helped and saved, sustained by trust in God and strengthened against the temptation of the Evil One and against anxiety over death. Thus the sick person is able not only to bear suffering bravely but also to fight against it. A return to physical health may follow the reception of this sacrament if it will be beneficial to the sick person's salvation. If necessary, the sacrament also provides the sick person with forgiveness and the completion of Christian penance.[7]

It is the whole person that the Lord wants to heal. Sickness of the body is just one manifestation of the need for healing. Of course, when the body is sick the person has a deep yearning for the

---

6   *Ibid* 1525
7   Rite of Anointing, 6

restoration of health. The person recognises, sometimes for the very first time, that health is one of God's great gifts to us. The Church has always prayed for "health of mind and body". We hear those prayers at every Mass. But many times we don't really pay attention. When a person experiences the blessing of being restored to health, he or she knows the experience of God's merciful love. But there is a deeper healing which God's mercy brings about in us and that is "the healing of the whole person". This is not just a physical healing, but a spiritual healing that brings great inner peace to one's whole being. As St Paul says, "Christ is our peace" (Ephesians 2:14). When we receive Christ in the sacrament of anointing and especially in the Holy Eucharist, he himself becomes our peace. Christ who is the mercy of God becomes our peace, not because we have merited this peace but because God wills to give us his peace in Christ. So, we can calmly and gratefully say, "The mercy of God is my merit". Being at peace with God, with oneself and with everyone in our life is the great transforming grace of God's mercy. As the Church celebrates the sacrament of anointing she confidently implores the Father of mercies for health of body, mind and spirit.

Proclamation of the word of God

The proclamation of the word of God is an integral part of the celebration of each sacrament. We may be more conscious of this proclamation during the celebration of Holy Mass, but in the celebration of the sacrament of anointing the priest also proclaims the word of God to the sick person and to the community of faith, even just a few that have gathered for the celebration. I always read the Gospel passage where Jesus invites us to come to him: "Come to me, all you who are overburdened, and I will give you rest" (Matthew 11:28). This is a very personal invitation that Christ is now extending to the sick person. We listen to this invitation; we accept it and, with our whole heart we gratefully respond and come to Christ for his rest. Listening to this personal word of Christ inviting us to come to him, to be one with him, opens our hearts to receive his gift of mercy and peace. Now we are ready to enter more deeply into the celebration of the sacrament. We have to listen in faith to what God is saying because without hearing his word we will not be able to enter into the mystery of the sacrament that we are about to celebrate.

Laying on of hands

Before the priest anoints the sick person he performs a very ancient liturgical gesture. He lays his hands on the sick person's head and prays silently. The Rite of Anointing explains the meaning of this gesture in this way:

> With this gesture the priest indicates that this particular person is the object of the Church's prayer of faith. The laying on of hands is clearly a sign of blessing, as we pray that by the power of God's healing grace the sick person may be restored to health or at least strengthened in time of illness. The laying on of hands is also an invocation: the Church prays for the coming of the Holy Spirit upon the sick person.[8]

The laying on of hands is the manifestation of the invocation of the Holy Spirit. We profess in the Creed, at Mass, that the Holy Spirit is "the Lord, the giver of life". When we invoke the Holy Spirit to come on the sick person we are asking the Lord, the giver of life, to fill the person with health and strength, with peace and tranquillity. The words of the hymn to the Holy Spirit capture this well:

> Come, O Creator Spirit come,
> and make within our heart your home;
> to us thy grace celestial give,
> who of thy breathing move and live.
> Our senses with thy light inflame;
> our hearts to heavenly love reclaim;

8   Rite of Anointing, 106

our bodies poor infirmity
with strength perpetual fortify.

The laying on of hands signifies that the Church is now invoking "the Lord, the giver of life" to come and fortify the sick person. When I have the occasion to anoint sick persons in their homes I always invite the whole family to gather around and lay their hands on the sick member of the family — on father, mother, son or daughter — and join in this great invocation of the Holy Spirit to come and fill their loved one with new energy and strength, with holiness and peace. I remind them that they are the ones who say "the prayer of faith" as we celebrate the sacrament: As the Rite of Anointing says:

> The community, asking God's help for the sick, makes the prayer of faith in response to God's word and in a spirit of trust. In the rites of the sick, it is the people of God who pray in faith.[9]

Notice that it is not just the priest who prays in faith. It is the community assembled for the celebration of the sacrament who make that prayer of faith. The family, gathered around their sick parent, brother or sister, should be encouraged to pray the prayer of faith with great confidence as they impose their hands on their loved one and pray for the merciful Father to pour out the Holy Spirit, the giver of life. This can be a moment of great healing for the family members as they prayerfully and with love impose their hands on their sick father or mother, brother or sister. It is a real experience of the mercy of God in their lives. It is also a prayer that brings great inner peace to the sick person, If a son or daughter, for instance, was alienated in some way from their sick mother or father and now, without a word, they gently impose their hands, or take their sick parent by the hand, as they silently pray, that wound of alienation in the parent's heart and in their heart is healed. In fact, the wound within all the family relationships is healed.

---

9   Rite of Anointing, 104

I always say to the sick person that God now wants him or her to surrender all anxieties, worries, fears, doubts, their whole past life into God's mercy so that they can use all their energy to fight the disease. The person at peace with God will have the inner strength to fight for life until the Lord calls him or her home.

Prayers of anointing

Having listened to Jesus' invitation to the sick person "to come to him" and having responded with the prayer of faith and the imposition of hands, the priest anoints the sick person. He can either use the oil that was blessed by the bishop at the Chrism Mass in Holy Week or he can bless the oil himself. I like to use this prayer of blessing of the oil because the words help to foster an expectant faith:

> God of all consolation, you chose and sent your Son to heal the world. Graciously listen to our prayer of faith: send the power of your Holy Spirit, the Consoler, into this precious oil, this soothing ointment, this rich gift, this fruit of the earth. Bless this oil and sanctify it for our use. Make this oil a remedy for all who are anointed with it; heal them in body, in soul, and in spirit, and deliver them from every affliction. We ask this through our Lord Jesus Christ.

That is a powerful prayer of blessing in which the Church concentrates the mind and heart of all present on God's merciful and healing love. We pray for healing "in body, in soul and in spirit" and we pray that the Lord will deliver the sick person from "every affliction". Now the sick person is ready to receive the anointing. The words are simple and direct. The priest, as he anoints the sick person on the forehead and the palms of the hands, says:

> Through this holy anointing may the Lord in his mercy and love help you with the grace of the Holy Spirit. May the Lord who frees you from sin save you and raise you up.

Notice that in the very moment of anointing, the Church appeals to the mercy of the Lord; "May the Lord in his mercy and love help you with the grace of the Holy Spirit". It is good for us to ponder what these words mean. Through the sacrament we enter into the mercy of God. In this sacramental moment we are at the "throne of divine mercy". We have come to Jesus who is "the face of the Father's mercy" and we are requesting the help of the Holy Spirit. Jesus reassures us with these words, "If you who are evil know how to give good gifts to your children who ask you, how much more will the heavenly Father give the Holy Spirit to those who ask him" (Luke 11:13). We are asking for the greatest of all healings: the coming of the Holy Spirit into our sinful hearts and lives. The Church reminds us, during Mass on the eve of Pentecost what the Spirit does in our lives, with this beautiful prayer during the Offertory:

> May the Holy Spirit coming near, we pray, O Lord, prepare our minds for the divine Sacrament, since the Spirit himself is the remission of all sins.

When we talk about the remission of our sins or the forgiveness of our sins we are talking about what the Holy Spirit does in our hearts. We could say that the very purpose of Jesus' life and death was that we would receive the Holy Spirit. He promised his disciples: "I shall ask the Father, and he will give you another Advocate to be with you for ever, that Spirit of truth whom the world can never receive since it neither sees nor knows him; but you know him, because he is with you, he is in you" (John 14:16-18). In response to this intercession of Jesus, the Father sent the other Advocate. He poured out his Spirit on the disciples. This is the mystery of Pentecost, the mystery of the Church.

The Second Vatican Council has made it very clear that the Church is established by Christ when the Spirit is poured out. We can fruitfully reflect on these texts of the Council:

By communicating his Spirit to his brothers, called together from all people, Christ made them mystically his own body.[10]

Rising from the dead, He sent his life-giving Spirit upon his disciples and through this Spirit has established his body, the Church, as the universal sacrament of salvation.[11]

After being lifted up on the cross and glorified, the Lord Jesus poured forth the Spirit whom he had promised, and through whom he called and gathered the people of the New Covenant.[12]

The Council teaches that the Church is the direct result of Christ's action of sending his Spirit. And, in our celebration of the sacrament of anointing we pray specifically for this coming of the Holy Spirit. That is why we pray with faith because Jesus is now interceding for us at the right hand of the Father and he is asking for this gift of the Spirit for us in this sacramental celebration. As the Rite says, "By this grace of the Holy Spirit the whole person is helped and saved."[13]

After the anointing of the sick person with the blessed oil, the priest, leads those present in more prayers for healing. This is my favourite prayer:

Lord Jesus Christ, our Redeemer, by the grace of your Holy Spirit cure the weakness of your servant... Heal his/her sickness and forgive his/her sins; expel all afflictions of mind and body; mercifully restore him/her to full health, and enable him/her to resume his/her former duties, for you are Lord for ever and ever.

The liturgical rite of the sacrament prepares the person for real openness to the Holy Spirit. All the elements of openness are there: the confession of our sins; the listening to the word of God; the

---

10 Constitution on the Church in the Modern World, 7
11 *Ibid*, 40
12 Decree on Ecumenism, 2
13 Rite of Anointing, 6

renewal of our faith in God's healing love; our willingness to receive a new gift of the Spirit. Whoever celebrates the sacrament with this openness always receives a great blessing. Even if it is not the blessing of physical healing, it will certainly be a blessing of inner healing. And, of course, sometimes the blessing of physical healing is also granted in this sacrament.

When we are celebrating the sacrament of anointing we believe that Christ himself is present, blessing the sick through "the prayer of faith" offered by those present, and filling them afresh with the Holy Spirit. We ask Christ with total confidence to heal the sick in body, mind and spirit.

Healing as wholeness

Healing means wholeness and wholeness is the effect of spiritual well-being, not just physical well-being. The athlete at his prime will be physically fit and robust in every way but if he is not at peace with himself he will not know the experience of wholeness, It will be just the physical dimension of his body, not the spiritual dimension, that is healthy and strong. St John Paul II pointed out, "The body can never be reduced to mere matter: it is a spiritualised body, just as man's spirit is so closely united to the body that he can be described as an embodied spirit."[14] That physical, strong body that we see is also an embodied spirit, and if the spirit is not at peace, no matter how strong the body may be, the person will lack wholeness. That is why the Church teaches us that in the sacrament of anointing it is "the whole person who is helped and saved." If, for instance, a selfish, arrogant, mean man goes into hospital with a cancerous tumour and comes out a selfish, arrogant and mean man, without a cancerous tumour, the cancer was cured but the person was not healed. On the other hand, if he came out of hospital a loving, kind, generous man, in a terminal condition, he would have been healed

---

14 St John Paul II's Letter to Families, 19

although the cancer was not cured. Healing is what happens in the whole person, not just in the diseased organ. And, as we know, the time comes when each person will leave this world and return to God. The happy death is the greatest healing.

Facing suffering with faith

None of us like to have to undergo suffering of any kind and yet we know, from experience, that suffering is part of human life. It is distressing to be with people while they are suffering, but it is so comforting to be with people who have found within their suffering a new grace of union with God.

In his encyclical on suffering, St John Paul II clearly states that suffering and death are evil, the ultimate consequence of original sin. Christ came to deliver us from this evil. In talking with Nicodemus Jesus said, "Yes, God loved the world so much that he gave his only Son, so that everyone who believes in him may not be lost but may have eternal life" (John 3:16). The ultimate evil would be the definitive loss of eternal life. St John Paul writes, "The only-begotten Son was given to humanity primarily to protect man against this definitive evil and against definitive suffering."[15] Christ, in his redemptive work, struck, as St John Paul II says, the "transcendental roots of evil" which are grounded in sin and death. "He conquers sin by his obedience unto death, and he overcomes death by his Resurrection."[16]

For those who accept his salvation, Christ has destroyed the eternal effects of sin, namely the loss of eternal life. But the temporal effects of sin, namely, suffering and death, remain in this world. St John Paul II writes:

> Even though the victory over sin and death achieved by Christ in his Cross and Resurrection does not abolish temporal suffering from human life, nor free from suffering

---

15 St John Paul II, *Encyclical on Suffering*, 14
16 *Ibid.*

the whole historical dimension of human existence, it nevertheless throws a new light upon this dimension and upon every suffering: the light of salvation.[17]

By dying he destroyed death

Christ enters into the world of suffering. He takes the suffering of the whole world upon himself. As the prophet foretold he was:

> A man of sorrows and familiar with suffering… and yet ours were the sufferings he bore, ours the sorrows he carried… he was pierced through for our faults, crushed for our sins. On him lies a punishment that brings us peace, and through his wounds we are healed (Isaiah 53:4-5).

Christ entered into the very heart of our world of pain and suffering and by his own suffering and death broke the power of sin and death for each of us. God had warned Adam and Eve that they were not to eat the fruit of "the tree of knowledge of good and evil" and that if they did eat of that fruit they "would most surely die" (Genesis 2:17). They were tempted by the evil one; they ate the fruit and they died. As St Paul said, "Sin entered the world through one man and through sin death, and thus death has spread through the whole human race because everyone has sinned" (Romans 5:12). The salvation that we have in Christ is not just the forgiveness of our sins but also the triumph over death. As we say in the Preface of the Mass of Easter Sunday, "By dying he destroyed our death, and by rising he restored our life." Jesus' resurrection from the dead is the ultimate sign of the redemption of our humanity because, it is in our humanity that he died, and in our humanity that he rose from the dead. As scripture says, "Since all the children share the same blood and flesh, he too shared equally in it, so that by his death he could take away all the power of the devil who had power over death, and set free all those who had been held in slavery all their lives by the fear of death" (Hebrews 2:14-15).

---

17 *Ibid* 15

Because Christ is at the heart of all human suffering we can speak of a "Gospel of suffering". St John Paul II writes:

> Down through the centuries and generations it has been seen that in suffering there is concealed a particular power that draws a person interiorly close to Christ, a special grace.[18]

Suffering in itself is not a good thing. But a good thing is concealed in suffering, namely "a particular power that draws a person interiorly close to Christ". When a person is united more intimately to Christ, through this special grace concealed in suffering, the whole nature of suffering is transformed. Indeed the person can then understand what St Paul meant when he wrote: "It makes me happy to suffer for you, as I am suffering now, and in my own body to do what I can to make up all that has still to be undergone by Christ for the sake of his body, the Church" (Colossians 1:24).

Christ's redemption is infinite. We cannot add to it. But at the same time, St John Paul II writes,

> In the mystery of the Church as his body, Christ has in a sense opened his own redemptive suffering to all human suffering. In so far as man becomes a sharer in Christ's history – to that extent he in his own way completes the suffering through which Christ accomplished the Redemption of the world.[19]

We can speak, therefore, of "redemptive suffering". Human suffering in and by itself has no redemptive value; we fight against suffering in every way we can. Human suffering, lovingly united to the suffering of Christ has a "redemptive value". As the Catechism says:

> By the grace of the sacrament of anointing, the sick person receives the strength and the gift of uniting himself or

---

18 *Ibid* 26
19 *Ibid* 24

herself more closely to Christ's Passion: in a certain way he or she is consecrated to bear fruit by configuration to the Saviour's redemptive Passion. Suffering, a consequence of original sin, acquires a new meaning: it becomes a participation in the saving work of Jesus.[20]

Those who refuse to unite their suffering with Christ on the cross can never recognise this value. It is a value which can be discerned only through the eyes of faith. It is a mystical value. That is why we should always pray for a renewal of faith for the sick person.

Without a renewed and a deepened faith the sick person may not be able to accept what the Church recommends in time of sickness: "The Church exhorts them [the sick] to associate themselves willingly with the passion and death of Christ (see Romans 8:17), and thus contribute to the welfare of the people of God".[21] Indeed, the "sustaining of trust in God" is considered one of the effects of the sacrament of anointing.[22]

We should participate in the celebration of the sacrament of anointing whenever we have the opportunity, even if the sick person is not a blood relative, because each sick person is our brother or sister. We should say "the prayer of faith" during the celebration of the sacrament with great confidence. For the sick, the anointing is the moment of their personal encounter with the Lord, the moment when they meet Jesus who shows them the mercy of the Father. We are there to support them in their faith; to encourage them to put their trust in God; to pray for their healing in body, mind and spirit; and to pray that in their suffering they will discover what St John Paul II described as "a special grace", namely "a particular power that draws a person interiorly close to Christ".[23] It is within this close union with Christ that the sick person experiences the full liberating grace of the mercy of God.

---

20 Catechism of the Catholic Church, 1521
21 *Rite of Anointing*, 5
22 *Ibid* 6
23 *Ibid* 26

Personal spiritual exercise

Centre yourself; sitting upright; breathing rhythmically; clearing your mind of all preoccupations.

Bring yourself to bodily stillness.

Now in your heart welcome the Holy Spirit, "the Lord, the giver of Life."

Invite the Holy Spirit to enter your whole being, especially into those areas where you may be lacking in health and energy.

Be still for some time in the presence of the God of mercy and compassion and receive his love.

Now focus again on your breathing as you relax in God's presence.

And bring yourself gently back to the world.

This spiritual exercise will deepen your awareness of being in the presence of the God of mercy and make you more grateful for the wonderful gift of the sacrament of the sick.

— Chapter Eight —

Mother of Mercy

One of the best loved and cherished antiphons to Our Blessed Lady is the Salve Regina, the Hail Holy Queen, in which the Church gives Our Lady the title Mother of Mercy. This antiphon is sung or said at Compline, the night prayer of the Church, from the Saturday before Trinity Sunday until the Friday before the first Sunday of Advent. For more than half the year then, in her official night prayer, the Church acclaims Mary as Mother of Mercy. It dates from around the twelfth century. Those who don't pray the liturgical prayer of Compline would know this prayer as the concluding prayer of the Rosary. We remind ourselves of the words of this ancient antiphon:

Hail Holy Queen, Mother of Mercy,
hail our life, our sweetness and our hope.
To thee do we cry poor banished children of Eve,
to thee do we send up our sighs,
mourning and weeping in this vale of tears.
Turn, then, most gracious advocate, thine eyes of mercy towards us and after this our exile show unto us the blessed fruit of thy womb, Jesus.
O clement, O loving, O sweet Virgin Mary.

St Alphonsus and *The Glories of Mary*

St Alphonsus de Liguori, a Doctor of the Church and Founder of the Redemptorist Congregation, one of the great Marian saints of the Church, based his most popular book *The Glories of Mary* on the Hail Holy Queen. This book has been translated into more than eighty different languages and appeared in more than eight hundred known editions. In his introduction he tells us modestly:

I leave to other authors to praise the other prerogatives of Mary and I confine myself, for the most part, to her mercy and the power of her intercession. I have gathered, as far as I was able (and it was the work of many years), all that the Fathers of the Church and the most celebrated authors have to say on the subject. I find that the mercy and power of Our Lady are admirably portrayed in the prayer Salve Regina (Hail, Holy Queen). Since all priests, secular as well as religious, are obliged to recite this prayer daily for the greater part of the year, I propose to divide and explain this beautiful prayer in separate chapters of this book. Over and above this, I thought Mary's clients would be pleased if I added some discourses pertaining to her principal feasts and her special virtues and if I incorporated devotions and pious practices which many of her servants have used and which have been approved by the Church.[1]

No book on Mary has been so widely distributed or so deeply appreciated as *The Glories of Mary*. Saints and scholars, learned and unlearned alike, have all found comfort and encouragement in this Marian classic. Alphonsus wanted the faithful to read the very best literature on Mary. That is why he worked for over twenty years gathering the material for his book. It is a work of immense scholarship and devotion. As Frederick Jones, in his biography of St Alphonsus wrote:

> Beneath the apparently devotional form of *The Glories of Mary* lies a rich mine of sound theological teaching on the Mother of God. As a positive contribution to the Mariological section of theology, it marked a decisive stage in the doctrinal evolution of the doctrine of Our Lady's Immaculate Conception.[2]

---

[1] St Alphonsus Liguori, *The Glories of Mary*, Liguori, Missouri, 2002, p. *Salve Regina* p. xxiii

[2] Frederick Jones, *Alphonsus de Liguori: The Saint of Bourbon Naples 1696-1787* (Dublin: Gill & Macmillan, 1992), 274.

St Alphonsus insisted that the members of the Redemptorist Congregation should always preach a sermon on Our Lady, the Mother of Mercy, during their parish missions and retreats. He knew from his own pastoral experience that when people hear a sermon or homily on the Mother of Mercy they are moved to open their hearts to receive the grace of conversion. Two hundred years later, the Second Vatican Council said: "Having entered deeply into the history of salvation, Mary, in a way, unites in her person and re-echoes the most important doctrines of the faith: and when she is the subject of preaching and veneration she prompts the faithful to come to her son, to his sacrifice and to the love of the Father."[3] The Council, like St Alphonsus long before, recognised the central role of Our Lady in the work of our salvation.

St John Paul II on St Alphonsus

St John Paul II, speaking about the legacy of St Alphonsus said:

> St Alphonsus is a gigantic figure, not only in the history of the Church, but for the whole of humanity as well. Even people who would not follow his vision, still see in him "the teacher of the Catholic soul of the West". He did for modern Catholicism that which Augustine accomplished in ancient times.[4]

In promoting love and devotions to Our Blessed Lady, St Alphonsus always focused on her tender mercy for all her children. In *The Glories of Mary*, he illustrates his theological exposition of Mary's wholehearted collaboration with her son Jesus in the work of our redemption by telling wonderful stories of how even the most hardened sinners received the special grace of conversion through the intercession of Mary, their Mother. Speaking to priests, nuns and seminarians in Naples, where St Alphonsus was born, Pope Francis said of *The Glories of Mary*: "In this book, I like reading

---

3   Constitution on the Church, 65
4   Cit. Alphonsus Liguori,: *Classics of Western Spirituality*, Paulists, New York, 1999, p.51

the stories about Mary that are at the end of each chapter; in them we see how Mary always leads us to Jesus."[5] Jesus, from the cross, commissioned his Mother to do precisely that, to be the Mother of all his disciples and to bring them all to him. Let us reflect on this scene on Calvary:

> Near the cross of Jesus stood his mother and his mother's sister, Mary the wife of Clopas, and Mary of Magdala. Seeing his mother and the disciple he loved standing near her, Jesus said to his mother, 'Woman, this is your son.' Then to the disciple he said, 'This is your mother.' And from that moment the disciple made a place for her in his home (John 19:25-27).

It is only in John's Gospel that we learn that Mary was on Calvary and that Jesus spoke to her. Matthew, and especially Luke, have a great interest in Mary's role as mother in the infancy of Jesus. But they didn't mention Mary's presence on Calvary. We are also struck by the fact that John's Gospel was written about sixty years after the death of Jesus. The writer tells us that he did not record everything that Jesus did and said: "The world itself would not contain the number of books that would have to be written" (John 21:25), "but these are recorded so that you may believe that Jesus is the Christ, the Son of God, and that believing this you may have life through his name" (John 20:31)... John is making it very clear, then, that Mary's presence on Calvary and Jesus' words to her are recorded so that we might believe. We cannot pass over this presence of Mary and these words of Jesus as if they had nothing to do with us. These living words of God, "this is your mother", are spoken to us today just as they were spoken to the disciple at the foot of the cross. We don't just hear the word but, as Jesus says, we "live on every word that comes from the mouth of God" (Matthew 4:4).

---

5   Catholic News Service, 16 April 2015

Mary's response

As we reflect on this Calvary scene the phrase "seeing his mother" is very significant. As Jesus looks on his mother from the cross, he sees not just his own biological mother; he sees the spiritual mother of his disciple, of his Church, which is coming to birth through his death and resurrection. Jesus sees in his mother a new maternity, a spiritual maternity. He reveals to his mother what he sees with the words: "Woman, this is your son." Mary didn't know that she was to become the spiritual mother of the disciple until God revealed it to her through the words of her dying son. Jesus' very last word to his mother is about her new relationship with his disciple. This is a revelation that Jesus is giving to his mother. And, just as Mary's response to the first revelation that the archangel Gabriel brought to her that she would become the mother of Jesus was, "Let it be done to me according to your word" (Luke 1:38), so now she makes that same response to this new revelation that Jesus gives her just before he dies: "Let it be done to me according to your word." Now Mary will live by this word of God spoken to her by her own son Jesus. By the power of that word of God, Mary becomes the mother of the disciple, the mother of all disciples.

Having seen a new reality, a new motherhood, in his own mother, Jesus then turns his gaze toward his disciple. What does he see in the disciple? Yes, he sees the disciple whom he loves, faithful at the foot of the cross. But he sees something else. He sees his brother. He sees one who has the same mother as himself. And he declares what he sees with the everlasting, creative word of God: "This is your mother." St Alphonsus writes,

> Here observe well that Jesus Christ did not address himself to John but to the disciple, in order to show that he gave Mary to all who are his disciples, that is to say to all Christians, that she might be their Mother. John is but the name of one, whereas the word disciple is applicable to all;

therefore our Lord makes use of a name common to all, to show that Mary was given as Mother to all".[6]

Some Protestant scripture scholars agree with St Alphonsus. The great Protestant scripture scholar Martin Dibelius wrote:

The beloved disciple is the person of faith, who has no need of proof (John 20:8). He is the witness to the mystery of the cross (John 19:35), and at the foot of the cross he becomes the son of Jesus' mother, thus representing other disciples who, in their relationship with God, have become brothers of Jesus.[7]

The disciple's response

Through the creative and redemptive word of Jesus, spoken from the cross, the disciple comes into a new relationship with his Master. The sign of that new relationship is that both are sons of the same mother: Jesus in his humanity is the son of Mary; the disciple in his redeemed humanity is the son of Mary. How does the disciple respond? John records, "From that moment the disciple made a place for her in his home" (John 19:27). John McHugh, a great expert on John's Gospel, wrote:

John 19:27 seems to demand a translation, which includes both the purely physical and the deeper, spiritual sense. "And from that hour the disciple took her into his own home and accepted her as his own mother, as part of the spiritual legacy bequeathed to him by the Lord".[8]

Benedict XVI agrees with McHugh:

The literal translation is stronger still; it could be rendered like this: he took her into his own – received her into his inner life setting.[9]

---

6 Alphonsus de Liguori, *Classics of Western Spirituality*, Paulists, New York, 1999, p.26
7 Quoted in Ignace de la Potterie, *Mary in the Mystery of the Covenant*, Alba House, New York, 1992, p.219.
8 John McHugh, *The Mother of Jesus in the New Testament* (London: Darton, Longman & Todd, 1975), 378.
9 Benedict XVI, Jesus of Nazareth, Part 2, Catholic Truth Society, London 2011, p. 221

The disciple made a place for Mary in his home, but more profoundly he accepted her, he welcomed her into his own life as his mother.

Reflecting on Mary's presence on Calvary the Second Vatican Council said:

> Thus the Blessed Virgin advanced in her pilgrimage of faith, and faithfully persevered in her union with her son until she stood at the foot of the cross, in keeping with the divine plan (see John 19:25), suffering deeply with her only begotten Son, associating herself with his sacrifice in her mother's heart, and lovingly consenting to the immolation of this victim who was born of her. Finally, she was given by the same Christ Jesus dying on the cross as a mother to his disciple, with these words: "Woman, this is your son" (John 19:26-27).[10]

Mary: the herald of God's mercy

In the hour of God's merciful redemption, Mary became the mother of all the disciples of Jesus. She became the Mother of Mercy. She was the herald of this mercy to her cousin Elizabeth. When Elizabeth, filled with the Holy Spirit, cried out, "Of all women you are the most blessed, and blessed is the fruit of your womb. Why should I be honoured with a visit from the mother of my Lord? For the moment your greeting reached my ears, the child in my womb leapt for joy. Yes, blessed is she who believed that the promise made her by the Lord would be fulfilled" (Luke 1:42-45). Mary responded to Elizabeth with her wonderful Magnificat in which she explains what is going on in her as:

> His mercy reaches from age to age for those who fear him.... He has come to the help of Israel his servant, mindful of his mercy... of his mercy to Abraham and to his descendants for ever" (Luke 1:50. 54).

---

10   Constitution on the Church, 58

Mary understands her pregnancy, the incarnation of her son Jesus Christ in her womb, as the act in which God remembers his mercy. And she will never forget, to use the words of Pope Francis,

> Jesus Christ is the face of the Father's mercy. These words might well sum up the mystery of Christian faith. Mercy has become living and visible in Jesus of Nazareth, reaching its culmination in him.[11]

As the Mother of Jesus, Mary gave birth to the "mercy of God incarnate". She suckled and nursed the mercy of God; she taught "the mercy of God incarnate" how to say his prayers as a child. And as Jesus "increased in wisdom, in stature, and in favour with God and men" (Luke 2:51), Mary continued to mother him. God had given her all the divine help she needed to be the Mother of his Divine Mercy.

Our Lady's presence in the Church

The disciple "makes a place for Mary in his home" (John 19:27). She is present as mother in the life of each disciple of Jesus. The disciple's response to her presence in his spiritual life is one of devotion; love and gratitude for her constant care; trust in her powerful intercession in times of need; great confidence in her as Our Mother of Perpetual Succour.

Our Lady is never absent from the Church nor from the experience of the faithful. As St John Paul II said:

> Mary is present in the Church as the Mother of Christ, and at the same time as the Mother whom Christ, in the mystery of Redemption, gave to humanity in the person of the Apostle John. Thus, in her new motherhood in the Spirit, Mary embraces each and every one in Christ, and embraces each and every one through the Church.[12]

---

11   Pope Francis, Bull of Indiction of the Extraordinary Jubilee Year of Mercy, 1
12   St John Paul II, *Mother of the Redeemer*, 47

Mary our Mother of Mercy embraces us with the divine love and mercy with which the Holy Spirit has filled her whole being in abundance. The motto of my Redemptorist Congregation is, "With him (Christ) there is plentiful redemption"; there is more than enough to go round. Mary is the mother of our redemption, the mother of mercy, the mother of Christ who is "the face of the Father's mercy". We can say, "With Mary there is plentiful mercy."

Spiritual motherhood

As our spiritual mother, Mary has a personal relationship with each of us. She is now body and soul in heaven and she knows each of us by name. She relates personally with each of us. You are not just one in a billion who calls on her for help. St John Paul II speaks very clearly about this unique relationship that Mary our mother now has with each one of us. It is a long passage but one that we should ponder for a long time:

> Motherhood always establishes a unique and unrepeatable relationship between two people: between mother and child and between child and mother. Even when the same mother has many children, her personal relationship with each of them is of the very essence of motherhood... It can be said that motherhood "in the order of grace" preserves the analogy with what "in the order of nature" characterizes the union between mother and child. In Christ's testament on Calvary his mother's new motherhood is expressed in the singular, in reference to one man: behold your son.

> It can also be said that these same words fully show the reason for the Marian dimension of the life of Christ's disciples. This is true not only of John, who at that hour stood at the foot of the cross together with his Master's mother, but it is also true of every disciple of Christ, every Christian. The Redeemer entrusts his mother to the disciple, and at the same time he gives her to him as his mother. Mary's motherhood

which becomes man's inheritance is a gift which Christ himself makes personally to each individual.[13]

The act of entrustment

Jesus entrusts each of us to the love and care of his mother. We honour him when we entrust ourselves to her. It is completely groundless to say, as some critics of Marian devotion say, that by putting our trust in Mary, the Mother of Mercy, we are failing to put our trust in Jesus. If Jesus didn't want us to have in our hearts the trust that a child has for his or her mother, he would never have proclaimed, in the solemn hour of our redemption, that Mary is our mother. We can turn to her in our every need and receive her maternal care.

On a priests' retreat years ago I was given this prayer to Our Lady, which I have said each morning ever since:

> Most Holy Virgin Mary, perfect disciple of Jesus, I come to dedicate my life and my priestly ministry to your Immaculate Heart. I desire to abandon myself to the will of Jesus, your Son, and walk in faith with you, my Mother. To you I consecrate my life in the priesthood. I give you every gift I possess of nature and of grace, my body and soul, all that I own and everything I do. Pray for me, that the Holy Spirit may visit me with his many gifts. Pray with me, that by faith I may know the power of Christ and by love make him present in the world.

You could adapt that prayer to your own vocation in life and say "I dedicate my marriage and my family life" or "I dedicate my life in my retirement" or "I dedicate this day to your Immaculate Heart". This kind of prayer of entrustment of oneself to Our Mother of Mercy is our grateful acceptance of the gift that Jesus gives to each of us when he says to us "this is your mother". We live by his last word from the cross.

---

13 *Mother of the Redeemer* 45

Asking Our Lady to intercede with the Spirit for us is surely a very biblical prayer. Mary was in the midst of the disciples praying for the outpouring of the Spirit on that first Pentecost day. Through her unique relationship with the Holy Spirit, the Son of God was born into this world as a human being; through this unique relationship the Son of God is born again in the hearts of those who turn to the Spirit through the intercession of Mary. We learn from Mary how to be open to the Spirit; we need her intercession to dismantle all those barriers we erect to the leading of the Spirit. A daily act of entrusting oneself and all one's needs and cares to Our Blessed Lady is a very good devotion to practise. The act of commitment can be very short: Totus Tuus, wholly yours, as St John Paul II had on his papal coat of arms.

Community and personal devotion to the Mother of Mercy

Devotion to Our Blessed Lady has been a constant feature of Catholic spirituality throughout the ages. It began when the disciple at the foot of the cross, "took her into his own – received her into his inner life setting".[14] The Church recognises that Mary so associated herself with Jesus on the cross that she suffered in her heart what he was suffering in his body. Mary became the mother of "the beloved disciple" in the awesome hour of the crucifixion of Jesus. As St John Paul II says:

> This "new motherhood of Mary", generated by faith, is the fruit of the "new" love which came to definitive maturity in her at the foot of the cross, through her sharing in the redemptive love of her son". [15]

Christ's faithful have always recognised that they have a special relationship with the Mother of Jesus, the relationship of sons or daughters to their mother, their mother in faith. And we have engaged in a great variety of different devotional practices to foster our relationship with our Mother of Mercy.

---

14   Benedict XVI, Jesus of Nazareth, Part 2, Catholic Truth Society, London 2011, p. 221
15   St John Paul II, *Mother of the Redeemer*, 23

Parishes played a leading role in promoting devotion to Our Blessed Lady. For many decades in most parishes there would be some form of weekly devotional service in honour of Our Lady. This developed within the Catholic community a profound trust and confidence in the powerful intercession of the Mother of Mercy, The most widespread and best known of these services for most of the twentieth century was the Perpetual Novena to Our Mother of Perpetual Succour. Many thousands of parishes throughout the Church held this weekly novena service. And millions of Catholics and other Christians were greatly blessed, encouraged and had their prayers answered.

In recent decades there has been a very great decline in the numbers of parishes having the Perpetual Novena or, indeed, any other devotional service in honour of Our Blessed Lady. This has been due to many social, cultural and religious changes. But the need for this powerful devotion to Our Mother of Perpetual Succour remains urgent. She is the Mother of Mercy. Our families need her perpetual help. Parents and grandparents experience an intense desire to pray for their children and grandchildren and they are looking for new ways in which they can support one another in this vital prayer of intercession to Our Lady.

Novena at home to Our Mother of Perpetual Succour

We need new forms of this much loved devotion. One new form is the Novena at Home. At this time, when the whole Church is being invited by Pope Francis to put the mercy of God at the very centre of our religious awareness we need to support one another in finding new forms of our traditional Catholic devotion to our Mother of Mercy.

In celebrating the Novena at Home you no longer have to go to your parish church for this time of prayer to Our Lady. You can do it in the privacy and comfort of your own home. And a special feature of this Novena is that we encourage you to invite a few friends and parishioners to share the Novena prayers with you. In this way you become, in the words of Pope Francis, "a missionary disciple". You assume your rightful leadership role in our Church, promoting a true devotion to the Mother of the Lord. In many ways the leadership for the development of true devotions in our Catholic communities has passed from the clergy to the laity.

Some of your friends and certainly some of the members of your parish will have a great love for Our Lady and they would jump at the opportunity of being able to share a weekly Novena, praying for their families, for their children and grandchildren.

Other friends and parishioners would be grateful for the opportunity to come together in a small community of faith, to pray for their own special needs. They could bring all their worries about their health or their financial situation to Our Lady. As they offer all these worries in prayer they will experience Our Blessed Mother's powerful intercession. That is why the Church calls her Our Mother of Perpetual Succour, Perpetual Help, always ready to help us.

Again, other friends would be very concerned about the state of the world and about the places in our world which are being ravished by terrorism of all kinds. They would welcome the opportunity to have a special time with Our Lady asking her to intercede for all those troubled places on our planet.

Through this Novena you would be able to unite your prayers with the prayers of millions of people all over the world who make this Novena to Our Mother of Perpetual Succour every week.

Hundreds of thousands of devotees of Our Lady find great inner peace as they join in the Perpetual Novena. You could begin your Novena any week. Homes are blessed, families re-united, health restored and strength given to face the challenges of life today as people seek the powerful intercession of Our Blessed Lady.

You will find all the details of the Novena at Home on our website: www.novena-at-home.redemptorists.co.uk

If you have no access to the internet some family member or friend will run off all the information for you.

Some well-loved prayers

From the very beginning of the Church the faithful called Mary "blessed" and turned to her in their time of need. Mary herself, in her great prophetic proclamation, her Magnificat, said "From this day forward all generations will call be blessed, for the Almighty has done great things for me" (Luke 1:48). St Luke's own community, where he was writing his Gospel, would have already been calling Mary blessed. You can't imagine St Luke writing those words, "from this day forward all generations will call me blessed", if his own community at the time were not doing so. We still say today a prayer to Our Lady that Christians as early as the third century were saying:

> We fly to thy patronage,
> O holy Mother of God.
> Despise not our petitions in our necessities,
> but deliver us from all dangers,
> O glorious and Blessed Virgin.

The earliest version of this prayer, written in Greek, dates from around 250 AD. Cardinal Shoenborn, commenting on this ancient prayer, writes, "The oldest versions of this prayer, written on papyrus, have a peculiar feature that is quite beautiful. They do not begin with 'we fly to thy patronage' but rather 'we fly to thy mercy, O Mother of God?'"[16] Even as early as the third century Christians were writing down their prayer to Our Lady and encouraging one another to "fly to her mercy". The Holy Spirit inspired in the hearts of the faithful, right from the beginning of the Church, the insight of faith that showed them that they should go to the Mother of Jesus and receive her protection and experience her mercy. Mary's mercy, of

16 Christoph Cardinal Shoenborn, *We Have Found Mercy*, Ignatius Press, San Francisco, 2012, p 119

course, is the mercy that God gives her in abundance so that she can show his great mercy to us.

We have that other wonderful prayer to Our Lady, The Memorare, much loved in our time by Blessed Mother Teresa:

> Remember. O most gracious Virgin Mary,
> that never was it known that anyone who fled to your protection,
> implored your help, or sought your intercession,
> was left unaided.
> Inspired with this confidence,
> I fly unto you, O Virgin of virgins, my Mother.
> To you do I come, before you I stand, sinful and sorrowful.
> O Mother of the Word Incarnate,
> despise not my petitions,
> but in your mercy, hear and answer me.
> Amen.

This is a very confident prayer to our Mother of Mercy. Those who say this prayer, especially in times of difficulties, experience Our Lady's swift response. This prayer has been handed on from generation to generation because the sentiments expressed here correspond to the experience of the faithful: "never was it known that anyone who fled to your protection, implored your help, or sought your intercession, was left unaided". What an extraordinary assertion of total trust in Mary's help. Notice that we are appealing to her mercy. Jesus said, "Be merciful, as your heavenly Father is merciful" (Luke 6:36). Mary lives by this word and shows us the great mercy she herself received from the Father when she was conceived without original sin, the wonderful mercy of her Immaculate Conception. Now, as our Mother of Mercy, Mary yearns to share that mercy with each of us. And, just as a mother gives her special care and attention to the sick child in the family so Mary has a very special care for each of us in our own weakness, whatever it may be. It is so important for us, then, to entrust to her motherly care all our weaknesses and all our sinfulness.

In what is surely our most popular prayer to Our Lady, and the one we would say most frequently, the Hail Mary, we implore Our Lady's intercession with these words, "Holy Mary, Mother of God, pray for us sinners, now and at the hour of our death". The importance of this prayer was indelibly imprinted on my mind three years before I was ordained a priest, when I had the grace to be with my family at home, saying the rosary around the bed of our father, as he was dying. My father had said the rosary at home every day of his life. My earliest memories as a boy at home is kneeling down with him and my mother, and with all my brothers and sisters (there were ten of us) saying the rosary together. Every day of his life my father had prayed to Our Lady, "Pray for us now and at the hour of our death." And now, at the hour of his death, we were praying the third Glorious mystery of the rosary, The Descent of the Holy Spirit, as he peacefully breathed his last.

These wonderful prayers to Our Mother of Mercy, that we have just considered, have been recited for many centuries in the Church and they eloquently testify to the faith and confidence of Catholic people in the powerful intercession of Our Blessed Lady.

Pilgrimages

Another manifestation of this great trust in Our Mother of Mercy is the practice of "going on pilgrimage". Pilgrimages to Marian shrines and places where Our Lady is said to have appeared provide millions of people each year with a vital source of devotion to Our Lady, a renewal of their faith and an experience of God's mercy. John Eade gave us some statistics about shrines and numbers of pilgrims:

> The last forty years have seen a vast increase in the numbers of Christian pilgrims. They travel to shrines dotted about Europe, the Americas, Africa and South Asia. Some of the international shrines are visited by several millions of pilgrims in a year – more than four million to Lourdes, five

million to Medjugorje, between three to four million each to Czestochowa and Fatima, many again to Guadalupe and Our Lady of the Snows in the Americas. A recent survey of Christian pilgrimages throughout the world identified about 8,500 active shrines.[17]

Nearly all the shrines are shrines of Our Lady. Most of the pilgrims are Catholic or Orthodox, though large numbers from the other Christian denominations, especially Anglicans, and even other world religions also visit shrines like Lourdes and Fatima, Knock and Guadalupe and Medjugorje. Pilgrims to any of the shrines where Our Lady is said to have appeared will have experienced the spiritual fruits of her presence. She always invites us to deeper faith through conversion and repentance, through prayer and fasting. Marian shrines are, first of all, places where we meet Christ in a new way; places for the celebration of the sacraments of Christ – the Eucharist, reconciliation, the anointing of the sick. Mary herself is never at the centre of the pilgrims' attention. But the pilgrims are at the centre of her attention. When Mary who took the initiative at the wedding feast in Cana said to Jesus "they have no wine", she then said to the servants, "Do whatever he tells you" (John 2:6). That is the word she has for all pilgrims. She is there to encourage them and to support them in doing what Jesus asks them to do. She never calls people to herself, she calls them to return to God and to open their lives to Jesus and receive the Father's mercy.

Marian shrines today are holy places where pilgrims receive the grace of deep conversions. They are challenged to take stock of the whole direction of their lives, to hear again Christ's call to repentance and discipleship, and to receive afresh the great gift of faith. Mary is always bringing the needs of her children to Christ: "they have no wine," "they have no peace," "they have no faith." At her shrines the pilgrim is assured that Mary is interceding for her children. But

---

17 John Eade, "To Be a Pilgrim," *The Tablet*, 6th August 1988, 995-96.

she is also giving them very specific directions. To each pilgrim she says, "Do whatever he tells you." We don't go on pilgrimage to Mary's shrines to escape from the commands of Christ; we go to be more faithful to his commands. And Mary, who certainly brings our needs before her son, brings his commands clearly to our minds.

Each summer, when I am on holiday at home in Ireland, I go with members of my family to Knock in the West of Ireland, where Our Lady appeared in 1879. Our spiritual routine is the same each year: we say the rosary in the Chapel of the Apparition; we celebrate the sacrament of confession in the Chapel of Reconciliation; we celebrate Mass for the pilgrims in the basilica and join the procession of the Blessed Sacrament after the Mass. The whole day is a celebration of the mercy of God which we experience as we honour Our Mother of Mercy.

Pilgrimages during the Jubilee Year of Mercy

Pilgrimages have always played a very significant role in the way the faithful celebrate Holy Years. Pope Francis, in announcing the Holy Year of Mercy is inviting us all to become pilgrims, seeking the great grace of the Jubilee of Mercy by going to a church or a shrine that the bishop has designated. He writes:

> I will have the joy of opening the Holy Door on the solemnity of the Immaculate Conception. On that day, the Holy Door will become a Door of Mercy through which anyone who enters will experience the love of God who consoles, pardons, and instils hope.

On the following Sunday, the Third Sunday of Advent, the Holy Door of the Cathedral in Rome – that is, the Basilica of Saint John Lateran – will be opened. In the following weeks, the Holy Doors of other Papal Basilicas will be opened. On the same Sunday, I will announce that in every local church, at the cathedral – mother church of the faithful in any particular area – or, alternatively, at the co-cathedral or another church of special significance, a Door of Mercy will be opened for the duration of the Holy Year. At the discretion of the local ordinary, a similar door may be opened at any shrine frequented by large groups of pilgrims, since visits to these holy sites are so often grace-filled moments, as people discover a path to conversion. Every local church,[18] therefore, will be directly involved in living out this Holy Year as an extraordinary moment of grace and spiritual renewal. Thus the Jubilee will be celebrated both in Rome and in the local churches as a visible sign of the Church's universal communion.[19]

During this Holy Year of Divine Mercy each of us will have the grace and the opportunity to join with the Church throughout the world in celebrating the mercy of God the Father, bestowed on us through Christ in the gift of the Holy Spirit. As we walk through the Mercy Door, in St Peter's, or in the cathedral church of our diocese, or in a shrine of Our Lady, or at another designated church, we believe that the Mother of Mercy accompanies us. With all her motherly heart she wants each of us to be filled with the mercy she sang about when she said to her cousin Elizabeth, "His mercy is from age to age to those who fear him" (Luke 2:50).

The moment Mary gazed for the first time on the face of her son Jesus she saw the mercy of God the Father. As Pope Francis says, "Jesus Christ is the face of the Father's mercy."[20] In the Hail Holy Queen we appeal to Mary with these words, "Turn, then, O most gracious advocate your eyes of mercy towards us." It is with those eyes of mercy with which Mary gazed on her son in the crib and on the cross, in the Resurrection and in his Ascension to heaven that Mary looks on each of us. She is not abhorred or shocked or dismayed by our sins or by our weaknesses. What she sees is her child in need of her help. And she is at our side to help. She is our Mother of Mercy, our Mother of Perpetual Succour.

---

18 The Local Church is the community of the diocese in which a person lives.
19 Pope Francis, Bull of Indiction of the Extraordinary Jubilee Year of Mercy, 3
20 Pope Francis, Bull of Indiction of the Extraordinary Jubilee Year of Mercy, 1

Personal spiritual exercise

Centre yourself; sitting upright; breathing rhythmically; clearing your mind of all preoccupations.

Bring yourself to bodily stillness.

Now in your heart welcome your Mother Mary as you say, Hail Holy Queen, Mother of Mercy.

In your heart entrust yourself, with all your worries and troubles, with all your sinfulness and weaknesses, to our Mother of Mercy.

Thank her for her Perpetual Help that she has given you.

Now be still in the presence of the God of mercy and allow Our Lady to "turn her eyes of mercy towards you".

Now focus again on your breathing as you relax in God's presence.

And bring yourself gently back to the world.

This spiritual exercise will deepen your awareness of being in the presence of the God of mercy and make you more grateful for the wonderful gift of Mary, your Mother of Mercy.